To MARK,

I hope you enjoy reading my book.

The Best!

WIN ONE FOR THE
$HAREHOLDERS!

AL ANGRISANI

To Lillian and Frank Angrisani—my mother and father—who taught me the value of common sense, education and hard work.

My sincere thanks to Sue Mellen, who helped me turn my thoughts and feelings into this tangible product. As we worked together to find the right words to define my years of experience in the turnaround business, we developed a true partnership and—more than that—a real friendship.

Thanks also to my friend John Kasich for believing in me and in this project enough to give his endorsement and write the eloquent foreword to this book.

And thanks to my colleagues (executives, managers and employees) from each of my turnarounds. They were the ones who made my model work; if not for their hard work, I would not be where I am today.

And finally, thanks to my family, for always being there for me over the last ten years, even while I lived in hotel rooms near the turnarounds and was not always available to them.

Foreword

Clarity in these Foggy Times

By Former United States Representative from Ohio, John Kasich, who served as Republican representative from Ohio, 1983-2001.

Author's note: No one is better suited to provide the foreword to this book than John Kasich, former U.S. congressman, political commentator, successful author and dedicated advocate for a balanced federal budget. This passage from Wikipedia illustrates how dramatically John has influenced federal budgetary policy.

"In 1995, when Republicans gained the majority in the United Sates Congress, Kasich was selected to become chairman of the House Budget Committee. As chairman, Kasich worked toward balancing the federal budget and was the chief architect of the Balanced Budget Act of 1997. As chairman of the Budget Committee, Kasich presided over the only U.S. budget surplus since 1969. In 1995, when Kasich assumed the position of budget chairman, the U.S. federal budget had a deficit of roughly $163 billion, and upon the conclusion of his tenure as budget chairman, the U.S. federal budget had a surplus of roughly $236 billion."

Win One for the $hareholders details why so many of America's once-great companies are failing and the common sense approaches to solving their problems.

Al Angrisani served in President Ronald Reagan's Administration as United States Assistant Secretary of Labor when I was a United States congressman from the great State of Ohio, and, while our paths never directly crossed in the 1980s, I had the great pleasure of getting to know him years later. Al and I have always seen eye-to-eye on how our nation's private sector impacts the lives of everyday Americans. We both come from hard-working, blue-collar families—his in New Jersey and mine in western Pennsylvania—who instilled in us values that have shaped our lives.

I have watched Al since he left Washington and have realized he has a sense for understanding how best to remedy what ails a company. His recent victory at Greenfield Online was his finest turnaround story yet. In fact, I am sure that the shareholders and investors would hail it as a masterpiece. Al was brought into Greenfield after it crashed from a $22 per share post-IPO high to $6 per share and falling. In two years, he not only turned Greenfield around, he reinvented it into a booming online media company. The success story was confirmed when Microsoft Corporation purchased Greenfield Online for $17.50 per share in October of 2008.

My last book, *Stand for Something: The Battle for America's Soul,* explored the constant struggle in our society between those who still adhere to the basic values that our mothers and fathers taught us and those who need to win at all costs. When we are all lined up at the starting blocks, who among us will hold true to those values when that gun goes off?

I know Al Angrisani manages to win while doing it the right way.

When Al is brought into a failing company, he brings with him the character and leadership I talk about in my book. More than ever, America and its corporate sector need answers and someone to help them step back from the cliff—back onto solid ground. Now, more than ever, we need new leadership, a proven business model and a renewed set of values that we can trust and lean on.

I am confident that the lessons in *Win One for the $hareholders* will give you someone to lean on, as it provides you with clarity in these foggy times.

Table of Contents

8   **Foreword**
Clarity in these Foggy Times
By Former United States Congressman, John Kasich

13   **Author's Note**

17   **I. Crisis in America**
Why are so many companies failing?

31   **II. Can this Company be Saved?**

43   **III. Understanding the Root Causes of a Failing Company**

59   **IV. Selecting the Turnaround Executive and Initiating the Turnaround**

77   **V. Introducing the Proven Model for Change**

The Proven Turnaround Model

93   **VI. Rightsize and Redesign the Business**

107   **VII. Grow and Optimize the Business**

123   **VIII. Exit and Maximize Shareholder Wealth**

139   **IX. In closing …**
Rising Out of the Ashes: A New Company with a New Value System

Author's Note

One of the best-kept secrets in the business world is the shareholder wealth that can be created through a properly executed turnaround of a troubled company. Bad news sells newspapers and cable subscriptions, so we hear more about corporate bankruptcies than we do about my favorite subject: the corporate turnarounds—happening right under our noses—that are maximizing shareholder value.

Today's *Wall Street Journal, New York Times,* CNBC and *Bloomberg Financial* are filled with stories about highly paid executives who have driven their companies into bankruptcy, while Boards of Directors did little or nothing to stop them from obliterating shareholder value. But when was the last time you saw a lead story about the successful turnarounds at HP, AT&T, Warnaco or any of a number of smaller public companies, including firms like Greenfield Online, my most recent turnaround? Collectively, these turnarounds have created many billions of dollars of new wealth for the shareholders, while also putting in place executives and Boards of Directors who create real value in these companies through knowledge, experience and hard work.

My objective in this book is to highlight the shareholder value that can be created from a properly executed corporate turnaround and to walk the reader through my proven, real-world model for executing a corporate turnaround.

I hope that, by the end of this book, the reader begins to see what I know: A troubled company that has been brought to the brink of bankruptcy is an opportunity for smart, hard-working investors and managers to build incredible wealth, while saving thousands of jobs and making America stronger.

I hope you enjoy the reading and that it inspires some new ideas.

Biography of Turnaround Expert and Author, Albert Angrisani

After completing the turnaround of Greenfield Online (formerly NASDAQ: SRVY), Albert Angrisani led the sale of the company to the Microsoft Corporation (NASDAQ: MSFT) for $497 million on October 13, 2008. Up to that point, Mr. Angrisani was President and Chief Executive Officer of Greenfield Online/Ciao, the world's largest provider of global consumer attitudes about products and services, via two distinct business units: web-based comparison shopping and Internet survey solutions. Mr. Angrisani joined Greenfield Online/Ciao in September 2005 after the company experienced operating and financial difficulties.

Prior to joining Greenfield/Ciao, Mr. Angrisani was President and Chief Operating Officer of Harris Interactive, Inc. (2002 – 2004), (NASDAQ: HPOL), a leading Internet marketing research company and parent of The Harris Poll™. By the end of his tenure at Harris, Mr. Angrisani led a turnaround that increased shareholder value by more than $200 million over the two-year period. Prior to joining Harris, Mr. Angrisani was President and Chief Executive Officer of Total Research Corporation (1999 – 2002), (NASDAQ: TOTL), which he merged with Harris Interactive after overseeing the company's turnaround and a $100 million increase in its shareholder value.

Mr. Angrisani served in President Reagan's Administration as the United States Assistant Secretary of Labor and Chief of Staff (1980 – 1984). As second in command at the Department of Labor, Mr. Angrisani managed $33 billion in annual budget outlays and 10,000 employees. A key accomplishment engineered by Mr. Angrisani was the creation of the Job Training and Partnership Act, a public and private partnership that saved billions of dollars and produced a more efficient federal training delivery system. In addition, Mr. Angrisani restructured the pension and welfare benefits administration and the federal unemployment insurance system. Prior to serving in the federal government, Mr. Angrisani was a Vice President of Chase Manhattan Bank in New York (1972 – 1980).

1 Crisis in America
Why are so many companies failing?

"**T**he stock market became an engine of doom, carrying to destruction the entire nation and, in its wake, the world. By July 8, 1932, the New York Times Industrial Average had fallen from two hundred twenty-four at the end of the initial panic to fifty-eight. U.S. Steel, the world's biggest and most efficient steelmaker, which had been $262 per share before the market broke in 1929, was now at only $22. General Motors, already one of the best run and most successful manufacturing groups in the world, had fallen from $73 to $8 per share. These calamitous falls were gradually reflected in the real economy. Industrial production fell by more than half from August 1929 to March 1933, while manufactured durables fell by 77 percent, nearly four-fifths. Business construction fell from $8.7 billion in 1929 to only $1.4 billion in 1933.

"Unemployment rose over the same period from a mere 3.2 percent to 24.9 percent in 1933 and 26.7 percent the following year. At one point, thirty-four million men, women and children were without any income at all, and this figure excluded farm families who were

1929

Excluding 1929 and the Great Depression, 2008 was the worst financial year in the history of the U.S.

also desperately hit. City revenues collapsed, schools and universities shut or went bankrupt, and malnutrition leapt to 20 percent, something that had never happened before in United States history, even in the harsh early days of settlement."

This passage from economist Paul Johnson's introduction to fellow economist Murray Rothbard's *America's Great Depression* ought to sound familiar, even to readers who aren't students of history. It could be describing the present-day corporate/economic landscape just as well as the late 1920s and early 1930s. Excluding 1929 and the Great Depression, 2008 was the worst financial year in the history of the U.S. Trillions of dollars of shareholder value were lost in the American public companies traded on exchanges. Just as in 1929 and into the early '30s, the stock market had again truly become "an engine of doom." And, just as in the late 1920s and 1930s, no one seems to know how to begin solving the calamitous problems. Rather than attacking the root of the tragedy— which I believe is corporate America's lost commitment to good, solid business practices and declining sense of responsibility to shareholders—the government simply throws billions of dollars at companies, hoping they will miraculously turn around.

If you need further proof of the crisis at hand, as I write this, all three auto companies;

perhaps one-third of all the banks in the U.S., including major forces in the financial sector; broker dealers like Lehman Brothers and Bear Stearns; insurance companies like AIG and thousands of other companies have all either gone bankrupt, are going bankrupt or are in serious financial trouble. And, just to add more fuel to the great economic pyre, the massive losses have extended to the intrinsic value of private companies, private equity firms and hedge funds and families and individuals that own those private companies.

From the top down, the federal government of the United States of America is a completely dysfunctional organization.

In short, we as a nation are teetering on the edge of a financial crisis of epic proportions. As predicted by Harry E. Figgie, CEO of Figgie International, a Fortune 500 company, in his book *Bankruptcy 1995,* "In 1995, the United States of America, as we know it today will cease to exist. That year the country will have spent itself into a bankruptcy from which there will be no return. What we once called the American Century will end, literally, with the end of the American way of life—unless you and I act now to pull ourselves and the country back from near certain oblivion." Figgie may have been a few years early with his predictions, but the scenario he described is certainly playing out today, with the experts suggesting the federal deficit for 2008 will exceed $1 trillion.

Even if we manage to dodge the bullet this time around, the seeds of collapse lie deep

From the bottom up, corporate America has lost its sense of purpose and direction.

within America. From the top down, the federal government of the United States of America is a completely dysfunctional organization making one bad decision after another. Our government simply does not work anymore! And, in my opinion, the problem began when the U.S. federal government embraced the concept of Keynesian economics and deficit spending, without mandated constitutional controls and limits on the amount of debt issued. This sowed the seeds of our current near-bankrupt condition, where politicians have no real accountability and access to an unlimited amount of debt through government printing presses—a formula for self-destruction.

From the bottom up, corporate America has lost its sense of purpose and direction. And it has devolved from a world leader in the twentieth century, building valuable products that generated wealth the hard way—through hard work and investment—to a nation of financial engineers who create unintelligible, transaction-based wealth around the concept of leverage and debt. In short, the fast buck and debt have won out over hard work and savings and the interests of shareholders.

Clearly, all too many corporate leaders have forgotten that their first and overriding responsibility is to safeguard wealth for their shareholders. With 60 percent of the American adult population invested in the markets in

2008, corporations have a direct responsibility to a large segment of the American public. And, indirectly, that responsibility extends to the whole population of the country—and the world—whose daily lives are dramatically impacted when corporate mismanagement leads to economic failure.

It's hardly a great leap to suggest that the current crisis could well echo the Great Depression, when, "City revenues collapsed, schools and universities shut or went bankrupt, and malnutrition leapt to 20 percent." Is this an exaggeration? Just ask California Governor Arnold Schwarzenegger, who in December 2008 suggested that the State of California could default on vendor, and possibly bond, obligations if the economic crisis of 2008 were to continue and fail to correct itself in 2009.

I sum the problem up as follows: All too many American businesses and the political infrastructure that makes the rules under which American businesses operate have developed an entitlement mentality. They've forgotten that it was a commitment to hard work, good business practices and responsibility to their shareholders that made this country great. Clearly, our founding fathers are turning over in their graves.

Our Leaders Have Failed Us!

The issue that bothers me the most about America's economic collapse in 2008 is how our political and business leaders have failed us as a nation. I have always had the utmost respect for the men and women who have risen to the top of government and corporate America, but that respect has been deeply shaken. To put it bluntly, arrogance, self-serving agendas and greed have replaced common sense, the interests of the people and the financial health of our nation as the rationale for decision making in Washington and on Wall Street. I was both surprised and pleased to see that our new president embraced that very issue in his inaugural address when he said:

What is required of us
now is a new era of
responsibility.

"Our challenges may be new. The instruments with which we meet them may be new. But those values upon which our success depends— hard work and honesty, courage and fair play, tolerance and curiosity, loyalty and patriotism— these things are old. These things are true. They have been the quiet force of progress throughout our history. What is demanded then is a return to these truths. What is required of us now is a new era of responsibility—a recognition, on the part of every American, that we have duties to ourselves, our nation and the world, duties that we do not grudgingly accept but rather seize gladly, firm in the knowledge that there is nothing so satisfying to the spirit, so defining of our character, than giving our all to a difficult task."

I truly hope he acts on his words!

Following President Obama's train of thought, if he is going to lead us to a new era of responsibility, we might say that the last eight years have been an era of irresponsibility, based on the current state of our economy. And, because responsibility, like leadership, starts at the top of any organization, we must look at the leaders who have failed us and ask ourselves why.

Starting with the government, President Bush, Vice President Cheney and the Congress inherited a federal budget in surplus from the Clinton Administration in 2000, thanks to the hard work of many people, including my friend John Kasich, who was chairman of the House Budget Committee during the Clinton years. In fact, in his eight years as president, Bush did not veto a single federal budget or spending bill, and as a result, presided over the largest annual federal budget deficits in our nation's history. This was completely irresponsible and was an intentional departure from the fiscally conservative principles of the Republican party. *As a card-carrying Republican and Reagan Administration veteran, I am asking myself how a Republican president could have spent us into a trillion-dollar budget deficit in 2008 that brought us to the brink of financial collapse.* Let me check my history books, but isn't the Republican Party supposed to be the guardian of taxpayers' hard-earned dollars and the party of fiscal responsibility?

	Deficit (In $ billions)	Surplus (In $ billions)
Start of Clinton Administration		
1992	290.3	
1993	255.0	
1994	203.2	
1995	163.9	
1996	107.4	
1997	21.9	
1998		69.2
1999		125.5
2000		236.1
Start of Bush Administration		
2001	144.5	
2002	409.5	
2003	589.0	
2004	605.0	
2005	523.0	
2006	536.5	
2007	459.5	
2008	1017.0	

(Figures from Wikipedia)

The result was predictable by many: an era of bankers gone wild.

Just imagine where we as a nation would be today if, instead of returning to deficit spending, the Bush Administration had continued the trend of building surpluses that they inherited from the Clinton Administration! In my opinion, the cumulative federal deficit could have been paid down to $6 trillion vs. the $12 trillion it is today, and the Dow Jones Industrial Average would be sixteen thousand instead of eight thousand today! History books will look back on the decision to return to deficit spending, after we turned the corner to surpluses, as one of the most irresponsible decisions made in the history of our nation. Our leaders were at the crossroads and they chose the wrong path; they failed all of us.

How could this flip-flop happen? Our leaders failed us because they allowed the agendas of special interest groups to replace the best interests and security of America's citizens. What in God's name were they thinking when they signed off on those deficits and relaxed or removed regulatory oversight of our nation's financial institutions and markets?

The result was predictable by many: an era of bankers gone wild making huge bonuses, selling bad mortgages and securitizing basically thin air, passing it off to unaware investors as quality-grade investments. By the way, the rating agencies and insurance companies that stood behind these thin-

Bouton, Chairman, Société Générale

re of risk-taking and weak internal controls enabled rogue
ôme Kerviel to run up more than $7 billion in losses at the
ank, forcing Bouton out as CEO.

Cayne, Former CEO, Bear Stearns

Stearns collapsed, its chief appeared to be clueless. Amid some
orst days of the crisis, he reportedly was off playing golf and

Fuld, Former CEO, Lehman Brothers

e his people hard and ignored warning signs, rewarding risk and
Nobody was more convinced that Lehman was too big to fail.

oodwin, Former CEO, Royal Bank of Scotland

the master of megamergers (ABN Amro), massive leverage, and
ic expansion. Then he dumped the mess on British taxpayers.
nder he's 'extremely sorry.'

Killinger, Former CEO, Washington Mutual

has a bank shown such brazen disregard for lending standards.
ger got rich while it worked. When home prices fell, WaMu went
ankruptcy.

el Ospel, Former chairman, UBS

lped make the Swiss bank one of the biggest subprime casualties.
ril, he said, 'The storm is passing.' In November, he called the
ion 'inconceivable to me until a short time ago.'

Schoonover, Former CEO, Circuit City

r mind the price wars, lousy service, and overbuilding. His worst
e was firing 3,400 of his most experienced employees in 2007,
ng they made too much money.

WIN ONE FOR THE $HAREHOLDERS!

air investment vehicles played as big a role in
bankers and politicians. In this vein, let's not f
appointed advocates of Fannie May and Fredd
prudent lending standards for mortgages to pu
everyone could afford a home—or a bigger and
home. There is plenty of blame to go around, b
leaders failed us and squandered away a governi
to replace it with a trillion-dollar annual budget
beyond, putting our nation in grave peril.

Moving to the private sector, the leadership failur
leaders and managers of many of our largest finan
January 19, 2009, *Business Week* article citing "The
the economic crisis of 2008 is a snapshot of the sit
text that follows was taken from the *Business Week* a

"With stock values plummeting and entire industrie
bets, it's hard to single out a handful of managers to

"The financial-services sector, for one, seemed like a
of reckless behavior once the U.S. housing market tu
Even some blue-chip firms seemed to forgo the basic
management amid an atmosphere of heady profits. A
later went to their governments, hat in hand, a numbe
remained oblivious enough to insist that they still dese
home millions in compensation. Investors responded,
those executives lost their jobs.

"Others managed to take a tough situation and make it
it was Sam Zell sucking the life out of an ailing media e
J. Schoonover gutting the morale of Circuit City's emplε
chain was losing sales, some leaders became paragons of
in a time of crisis. Here is *BusinessWeek's* Dirty Dozen of

Martin Sullivan, Former CEO, American International Group

With his constant assurances on AIG's health, it was clear Sullivan didn't keep an eye on the shop. Hank Greenberg had his faults, but he knew what was going on.

Richard Wagoner, CEO, General Motors

He inherited a mess, but he did little to invest in fuel-efficient cars and force radical change. And flying to Washington on a private jet to request money? Not smart.

Jerry Yang, CEO, Yahoo!

Microsoft made an offer to buy his company and Yang walked away. Discussions with Google fell apart and the share price plunged. Yang's best move: announcing that he's looking for a replacement.

Mike Zafirovski, CEO, Nortel

From accounting restatements to failed restructurings, it's hard to believe the Canadian telecom was once worth $250 billion. Zafirovski came to clean it up. Shares cost $15 a year ago. Now they're 25¢.

Sam Zell, CEO, Tribune

In one year, the self-described grave dancer and Chicago real estate baron went from promising to save the newspaper business to orchestrating the largest print media bankruptcy ever."

I believe that history will show that the leaders of these failed institutions and many others forgot the basics of risk vs. reward and performance vs. reward as they related to their companies and their own compensation. I suspect they never calculated the possibility of an economic failure into any of their decisions to lend and invest outside prudent risk parameters. To me, that is the height of irresponsibility because, given the leverage they applied to the balance sheets of their organizations, an economic failure could only result in the failure or collapse of the organizations they managed. To put it another way, it would be the equivalent of the head of a household going to Las Vegas and gambling all of the equity in the family home at the craps table, knowing that failure would result in his or her family being homeless.

To add insult to injury, while they were gambling away franchises that took generations to build, they were paying themselves hundreds of millions of dollars in bonuses and compensation. How do you honorably pay yourself that much money for wrecking a company? Where is the historical relationship between performance and reward that has driven wealth creation in America since its inception? Where were the Boards of Directors of these companies and the respective Compensation Committees? It's another subject, but one cannot ignore that the basic governance structure of large public companies is broken and needs to be fixed with new and better regulations and oversight.

When we look back over the economic collapse of 2008, I believe one cause for the disaster will stand out above all others: The leaders of our government and business sector did not act in the best interests of the taxpayers and shareholders. These leaders brushed aside the sacred responsibility that comes with their respective offices to the taxpayers, investors, employees, citizens and a host of other stakeholders and replaced it with other loyalties, including their own self-interest—and, of course, there was more than a little stupidity mixed in with all this.

So, when President Obama speaks of, "a new era of responsibility" to correct America's ills, it's clear he and I see the problem in the same light. As you read on, you will also see that responsibility is one of several major themes woven into my turnaround model and repeated throughout this book.

This book is all about revitalizing that sense of commitment/responsibility to good business practices and shareholders—a necessary step if we are to avoid an economic collapse destined to rival the Great Depression in severity. My system for fixing broken companies and cleaning up the mess created by leaders who make bad decisions is a battle-tested, real-world approach to bringing a company back from the brink of collapse. My turnaround model and the work I do fixing companies is real and founded in proven business practices developed specifically for companies in crisis.

The leaders of our government and business sector did not act in the best interests of the taxpayers and shareholders.

In my work, if I get it wrong the company goes out of business—period! I am the last line of defense—the barrier that protects shareholders and thousands of people employed by the company and their families from lost jobs and income and the pain that comes from that experience. And, believe me, I know that pain because I lived it as a child. In fact, I think it's a deep understanding of that overwhelming pain that has led me to the work I do—which is really all about helping companies live up to their responsibility to the people who count on them. And it has been the driving force behind my decision to write this book. I hope that, through my work and this book, I can reach corporate leaders across America. Together, we can save scores of companies from failure, and spare shareholders and families inestimable suffering. So, please read on.

2 | Can this Company be Saved?

> **"If you don't know where you are going,**
> **any road will get you there."**
> — Lewis Carroll, in *Alice's Adventures in Wonderland*

The above quote is the perfect place to begin a discussion of the way I've learned to approach turnarounds after twenty years in the business.

Every time I walk into a company that I'm considering taking on, I feel like *Al* in Wonderland. Invariably, the company is in a confused state somewhere between fantasy and reality—just like the mythical land Carroll created for Alice's adventures. And, like Alice, the company leadership can't find its way out of the rabbit hole and tunnel they've wandered down into.

When I travel down a troubled company's rabbit hole, here's what I find: a business that is spiraling out of control. The sales organization is selling against the house, losing—rather than making—money on every sale; the operations group is processing work that is unprofitable; the leadership is in denial, looking for shortcuts or playing golf while the company sinks deeper down the rabbit hole, and shareholders are in a state of panic over lost wealth. I think you get the picture.

My job—which, like Alice's journey, is always an adventure—is to quickly restore the truth and bring an absolute sense of reality to the situation at hand. How do I do it? Through a powerful mix of crisis-management experience, a proven turnaround model, a precisely crafted plan for the unique situation and a sense of urgency that creates a straight line from point A to point B and out of the rabbit hole. My goal, and the new reality of the company, when it comes out the other side of my process, is restoration of the equity value for existing shareholders through new profits and the new cash generated from their once broken and lost company.

I cannot emphasize the next fact enough: Although I am very good at what I do, not all companies can be saved or turned around. In fact, the most critical decision I make in the turnaround process is the very first decision— the decision I make before the process even begins: the judgment call on the survivability of the company. In short, I have to determine the company's level of stress. If a company is under debilitating stress, moving it into either distressed or bankrupt territory, it may be beyond my help.

All TUC-kered Out

Professionally, I focus on companies that are not yet distressed and that can be saved from the world of bankruptcy or worse—going out of business. These companies are what I like to refer to as **TUCs** or *troubled and under-performing companies*. Basically, these are companies that have lost their way on the corporate superhighway—with their bottom lines and shareholder value impacted by the detour—but can still find their way back onto the right road. If a company has temporarily lost sight of, but not abandoned, good business basics, has a supportive Board and dedicated management team AND a market (both clients and the industry at large) that is receptive to its products and services, it can often be saved.

The process of making the decision as to whether or not a company can be saved is complicated and time-consuming. (I will discuss my decision-making process in detail later in the book.) I often spend sixty to ninety days intensely analyzing a target TUC before entering negotiations with the Board of Directors relative to acceptance of the assignment and terms of engagement. However, before I conduct a detailed business, financial and operational analysis of the

Although I am very good at what I do, not all companies can be saved or turned around.

company—which includes interviews with accountants, lawyers, the executive management team and customers—*there are some absolute indicators of success that must be present for the turnaround to be possible. I view these indicators as hidden assets because they are generally invisible to the untrained eye.* After more than twenty years as a turnaround practitioner, I have learned how to recognize the signs that a company has what it takes to undertake the grueling work of a turnaround and come out whole on the other side. It's the presence of these hidden assets that—like reinforced battle armor—gives me the courage to take on the battle for survival that is every turnaround.

Stealth Identification of Hidden Assets: The Turnaround CEO's Secret Weapon

Before I enter into the detailed analysis of the TUC (which I'll explain in Chapter Five), I conduct a quiet and almost stealthy search for the hidden assets of the company that have been lost in the turmoil of the company's failing performance. I usually find these assets through interviews conducted with the executive management team, second-tier management team and key clients.

I begin each interview by explaining that my model doesn't require that I replace management. Obviously, that allays a huge fear and puts managers at ease. I then explain that I'll provide a system and environment where their talents will be recognized and they'll thrive. In turn, a partnership forms, with honesty at its core. Managers begin to talk about the company's real problems and opportunities—issues we resolve to tackle together. They especially love talking about all the good ideas, products, opportunities and technologies that have been squandered while the CEO and leadership team were hunkered down in their bunkers. These interviews give me an understanding of the true workings of the company, which cannot be found on the financial statements or due diligence documents, helping to uncover the hidden assets that are essential to the turnaround's success. Those assets, which I must uncover before moving on to a deeper analysis of the troubled company, are as follows:

1. It's All About Management Commitment:
Starting from the top down, the Board of
Directors and executive management team,
the generals in the impending war, are rooted
in reality and realize they are losing the war.
They must be willing to make the necessary
sacrifices to win the war. These sacrifices
include surrendering operational control of
their business to me as the *change agent* (a term
we'll define a little later in the book). It also
means accepting personal accountability as a
team for the results of the turnaround going
forward, reflected in a reasonable change in
compensation and roles and responsibilities
within the team.

They must be willing
to make the necessary
sacrifices to win the war.

If the company is to have a chance at
survival, the entire management team must
be committed to the success of the company.
That means that all managers must see the
turnaround as an opportunity to prove
themselves. Carrying this idea further into
the organization, the second tier of executive
management must go from seeing no future
with the company to having a shot at becoming
front-line management, as the turnaround
CEO tests the top-tier management team. This
second tier is usually younger and a source of
great energy for the effort.

2. Cash is King: There must be sufficient
wasteful spending buried in the inherent
cost structure of the company to allow me—
through expense reduction—to achieve neutral

or positive cash flow from operations in the first stage of the turnaround.

A second cash criterion (or hidden asset) is the longer-term ability to generate sufficient cash from operations to eliminate or substantially reduce long-term debt and de-leverage the company.

In short, cash and the ability to generate new cash from operations are, next to the intellectual and human capital in the company, the most valuable assets of a turnaround.

3. Creativity at Its Core: The business model and products can be reconceptualized into a newer and more relevant concept for clients, markets and investors to embrace. The intellectual capital of the company—reflected in new technology, research and development, and new product ideas—that has been ignored in troubled times becomes critical to re-energizing sales, market perception, organization dynamics and investor interest.

4. Customers First: The brand of the TUC may be tarnished, but it is the repository of years of success and can quickly come to life as the TUC's performance and marketplace presence improves. Finally, the not-so-happy customer base built up through years of successful operation can quickly become a loyal customer base again as the company gets back on its feet.

Creativity at Chrysler

In "The Chrysler Story" chapter of *Iaccoca an Autobiography,* Lee Iaccoca writes that he knew when he arrived on the scene at the automaker in September 1979, that Hal Sperlich, head of Product Planning, had been working on the K Car since 1977. In fact, he admits that the car's development history actually goes back to the time in the mid-70s when he and Sperlich worked together at Ford and wanted to build the car. He knew that, given the oil shock of the late 1970s, the world was going to want smaller, more efficient cars and that the K Car fulfilled that need perfectly. The new K Car product was quietly built into the overall Chrysler turnaround plan and, as history has shown, it was the true pivot point for the incredibly successful turnaround. To say the least, the K Car was a hidden asset at Chrysler that the old leadership team was ignoring and that the competition was clueless about. Iaccoca knew how to pivot upward on this incredible hidden asset in a company that was bankrupt.

This is an example with which you'll be able to identify as I walk you through my turnaround model and process. It is THE perfect example of incisive new leadership using a hidden asset—which had been previously ignored—to help rescue the company.

5. In the Wild Card Category: There are no legal, regulatory or major external issues that could emerge and rear their ugly heads, thus undermining a successful operational and financial turnaround. Such hidden beasts might include class action litigation, SEC and IRS problems, or intellectual property concerns.

The rabbit holes I never try to crawl down to effect a turnaround are the ones marked **Distressed or Bankrupt** (See definitions at the end of this chapter). The leadership of these companies has ignored the problem too long, and, in my opinion, a turnaround focused on restoring value to existing shareholders is either impossible or so high in risk that it is not worth my time. My time can be better spent on the TUCs, where leadership has recognized the problem at hand and supports me in fixing the problem for shareholders. Hewlett Packard (HP) is an excellent example of a large TUC that, in 2004, lost its way. But the Board of Directors and leadership of the company recognized the problem and developed a turnaround effort before HP became another distressed (near-bankrupt) or bankrupt technology company.

Finding Its Way Out of the Rabbit Hole

Figure 1

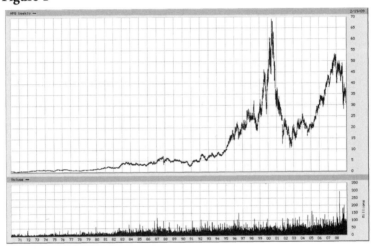

The stock chart tells the HP story perfectly, as it shows a company with unbridled success from 1965 to 2001, with the stock price rising from $2 to $80 on strong growth and profits. In the 2001 to 2004 timeframe, global competition, new products, poor management decisions and a host of other problems caused HP to start the downward decline of growth and profits that drove the stock to under $20 per share. This was the key inflection point at which the Board of Directors had to choose whether to delude itself and not recognize the problem, or make a bold change of leadership and direction to save the TUC and avoid possible bankruptcy.

Instead of deluding itself, the Board made a leadership change and brought in Mark Hurd to lead a turnaround effort. Hurd first succeeded CFO Robert Wayman, who had served as interim CEO from February through March 2005. Then, in September 2006, when non-executive chairperson Patricia Dunn resigned, Hurd was named her successor. He now sits as chairman, CEO and president of the company.

Hurd had previously spent twenty-five years at tech giant NCR, serving as CEO and president during his final two years. Bringing in Hurd was a stroke of genius by HP's board; his leadership of NCR was marked by successful efforts to improve operating efficiency, bolster the position of NCR's product line and build a strong leadership team—all critical moves for a TUC. In fiscal 2004, NCR and Hurd generated revenue of $6 billion, up 7 percent from a year earlier, and net income rose nearly fivefold to $290 million!

At HP, Hurd immediately laid off 10 percent of the workforce, eliminated contributions to the pension plans of U.S. employees and divided the business into seven new entrepreneurial business groups. Reflecting on his actions, Hurd said, "Our objective was to lay out a simpler, nimbler, more efficient HP." In short, he quickly brought a sense of urgency and reality to HP that put it back on the road to recovery, rather than allowing it to continue its downward spiral into bankruptcy.

Today, HP growth and profits have recovered, along with its stock price, even in the dismal stock market of 2008.

Definitions of TUC, Distressed Company and Bankrupt Company

■ Corporate Stress Levels

Bankruptcy: The most extreme level of stress, this involves a legal proceeding for a company that is unable to pay its outstanding debts. Bankruptcy proceedings in the U.S. can fall under several chapters of the Bankruptcy Code, ranging from a complete liquidation of assets as outlined in Chapter 7, to a thoughtful reorganization of the business and its financial and operating infrastructure as defined in Chapter 11. In all of these cases, the underlying equity and debt in the company are essentially worthless. This is a poor environment for a business turnaround which, for our purposes, is focused on restoring shareholder value for the current shareholders. The following is a list of the five largest bankruptcies in history:

1. Lehman Brothers, $639 billion in assets
2. Worldcom, $103 billion
3. Enron, $63 billion
4. Conseco, $61 billion
5. Texaco, $35 billion

Distressed Companies and Securities: This is the level of stress in a company that is near, but has not entered, bankruptcy. At the distressed stage a company is having great difficulty meeting its financial obligations, and, as a result, the underlying equity and debt in the company have suffered substantial reduction of value and are at risk of default. However, these obligations are not worthless and trade largely through the *vulture investors* and *bottom-fishing* funds and organizations specializing in *special situations.* This, like the bankrupt company described above, offers a bad environment for a business turnaround. However, while an operating and financial turnaround of a business at this level of stress is very risky, it is possible. The following is a list of companies that are currently distressed, but not bankrupt:

1. Three auto companies: GM, Ford and Chrysler
2. Best Buy—as opposed to Circuit City, which just went into Chapter 11 Bankruptcy
3. XM Satellite Radio
4. Krispy Kreme Donuts

Troubled and Under-performing Company (TUC): This is the level of stress in a company that is experiencing severe and sustained financial and operating performance, which have significantly impacted its public stock price or underlying equity valuation. The company is at the *point of inflection,* where it needs new leadership and a new plan to reverse the decline and where failure to act will cause it to become a distressed company, unable to meet its financial obligations. This is the world where I live and the one I will explain in this book.

Reborn companies like HP understand that, before a successful turnaround can be implemented, it's critical that a business understand how it got into this supremely uncomfortable position in the first place—so it can avoid a recurring case of *deja vu* all over again. Then, once a company has a thorough understanding of how it wandered into the quicksand surrounding it, it can insert the right turnaround agent into the turnaround process.

3 | Understanding the Root Causes of a Failing Company

I n these days of complex, global businesses and markets, it's far too easy for even the best Boards of Directors and management teams to make mistakes that start a company on the road to becoming a TUC. If these missteps are caught and corrected in time, the company can be set back on its feet. But, if these problems are allowed to grow and compound, treatable injuries become fatal traumas, leading to bankruptcy—or even complete failure.

The development, or devolution, of a TUC is rooted in both strategic and tactical mistakes by a company. They are usually connected but difficult to sort out when trying to figure out what ent wrong at the company and how to fix the problem. My proach is to start with an analysis of the tactical, or executional, t causes and follow them like a trail back to the bigger, strategic causes that preceded the tactics—perhaps years before the any became a TUC. Based on my experience analyzing s, the root causes of a TUC generally fall into a few major ts. What amazes me most, and could be the subject of a

What amazes me most is that everyone keeps making the same mistakes over and over again.

study of CEO and Board behavior, is that everyone keeps making the same mistakes over and over again.

Here are the common tactical root causes of a TUC:

1. Failed merger and acquisition activity, usually manifested in the inability to integrate the acquisition and realize the benefits assumed with the acquisition. The result is an over-leveraged balance sheet, drain on cash from operations to debt service vs. reinvestment in the business and loss of control of the core competencies of the business: sales, operations and technology.

Merger Madness

A good example of a company that has fallen prey to this hazard is Yahoo!. Over the past five years, from 2003 to 2008, Yahoo! has acquired forty-two companies, at a great cost to its shareholders. According to The Daily Deal, the total cost to shareholders of fifteen of the companies was $4.7 billion, with the remaining twenty-seven having been acquired at an undisclosed price. During this same period, Yahoo!'s stock has declined from a high of $100 per share to $12 today. The bottom line here is that Yahoo! acquired these companies and failed to integrate them into normal business operations in a manner that generated more profits and more shareholder value. Instead, like Time Warner and so many other companies who promise shareholders more profits from merger and acquisition activity, the result is less profit, more debt on the balance sheet and a lower stock price.

In my opinion, the reason for this failure to integrate is poorly thought-out operating details pre-acquisition and no accountability within the acquiring corporation once the acquisition is done. Everybody wants to be the hero, putting the deal together and announcing it to shareholders and Wall Street, but nobody wants to do the years of hard work integrating the new company into the operating and financial infrastructure of the parent company.

Doing it Right

An example of M&A activity done the right way is EMC, the data storage/information infrastructure giant. Joe Tucci became CEO in 2000 and was promptly greeted by the bursting of the Internet bubble and the dot-com crash. The next year, the company sustained an earnings loss of $508 million on approximately $2 billion of revenue.

Overnight, EMC became a TUC, and Tucci had to oversee a turnaround similar to the type we are talking about in this book. Fortunately, he developed his turnaround skills at Wang Labs, when he successfully pulled it out of Chapter 11 bankruptcy protection in 1991. At EMC, Tucci swung into action, rightsizing the company by eliminating nearly one-third of the workforce and streamlining expenses to accommodate the collapsing revenue line as dot-coms stopped buying equipment.

At the same time, Tucci started to rebuild the revenues of the company by diversifying into new products in the software and managed stored data sectors. He did this through new product development and acquisitions that were properly integrated into the core storage hardware business of EMC. In fact, you might say that EMC is universally obsessed with integration. The mantra *One EMC* is a theme running through all company communications—internal and external—and finds its way into every corporate presentation.

The strategy worked, and by 2003 EMC had reversed $500 million in losses into $500 million in profits. On the acquisition side, Tucci bought data management software companies Legato Systems and Documentum. Then came VMware, which sells software that makes computer servers more efficient. By 2005, thanks to properly purchased and integrated acquisitions and efficient operations of the core business, EMC profits grew to $1.2 billion on revenues of $9 billion. Between 2005 and today, EMC has completed several more acquisitions and has grown profits to $1.7 billion on $13 billion in revenues.

EMC's stock price is flat to down today like so many other companies that are suffering from the market crash of 2008, but there is no doubt that EMC knows how to successfully purchase and integrate acquisitions to drive growth of bottom-line profits. No turnaround help will be required at EMC for the foreseeable future.

2. The breakdown of essential checks and balances in the relationship between the Board of Directors and CEO. As British historian Lord Acton accurately pointed out: "Power tends to corrupt and absolute power corrupts absolutely." When the CEO becomes too powerful, the results can be devastating. A successful company is a team with a leader but not a dictator. The Board of Directors is the custodian of shareholder value, so when it does not play an active enough role in the oversight of the company, it is not living up to its major fiduciary responsibility. In this case, mistakes occur that can have an overwhelming effect on shareholder value and overall business health.

The business landscape is littered with U.S. corporations that have failed because of excessive CEO power and its handmaiden: greed. Companies in every industry have failed—and continue to fail—because the person at the top wanted the rush that comes from unfettered power and a few more million in a bank account. Enron, WorldCom, Bear Stearns and Global Crossing are just a few good examples. As John Kasich, an architect of President Clinton's balanced budget, wrote in his book, *Stand for Something: The Battle for America's Soul,* "What these folks did at Enron and WorldCom was wrong. Dead wrong. It had a cataclysmic impact on corporate America—not just at the companies involved but across the board. It hurt people, communities, job creation, families and wounded our economy. All because a few people wanted to earn a couple million dollars. And of course it ultimately destroyed those few people as well."

The message is clear, every CEO must be accountable to and share power with the Board of Directors or big—maybe fatal—mistakes are bound to be made.

When the CEO becomes too powerful, the results can be devastating.

The following is a perfect example of failed checks and balances.

Driving Toward Trouble at General Motors

It was a clear signal that General Motors was headed for trouble when Ross Perot left its Board of Directors. While a maverick and highly opinionated, Perot is great to have around the boardroom in any tough situation. Because of his ramrod strength, he provides just the right counterbalance to a CEO—who is apt to be just as opinionated. A board member like Perot isn't afraid to challenge a CEO, ensuring that important strategic decisions are the right ones. We're talking here about life-and-death decisions that often involve large amounts of capital belonging to the shareholders. When the Board of Directors becomes a rubber stamp or lapdog for the CEO, that company is headed for trouble.

In GM's case, company leadership knew there were problems but hadn't the will to make necessary changes. As Wall Street guru Maryann Keller wrote in "Why Companies Fail" in the November 14, 1994, edition of *Fortune,* "GM's bosses recognized the need to shake up the company and operations but, over the years, had built up such an intricate bureaucracy that change and progress took an eternity."

It may have been the smartest move of his career when then-CEO Roger Smith engineered the purchase of Perot's data processing company, EDS, which gave Perot a place on the GM Board. But, all too soon, it became clear that GM's "intricate bureaucracy" and Perot's maverick style were like oil and water. *At one point, Perot said of the overblown GM establishment, "When we find a snake at EDS, the first thing we do is kill it. At GM, the first thing you do is set up a committee on snakes. Then you bring in a consultant who knows a lot about snakes. The third thing you do is talk about it for a year."*

Eventually, tension grew to a fever-pitch; GM bought Perot's GM shares and ousted him from the Board. Since that time, twenty years ago, I believe GM's decline has been inevitable.

Roger Smith and all the GM CEOs who have succeeded him have not been strong enough to change the culture. I believe that Perot was and—because he posed a threat to the corporate status quo—was jettisoned from the Board. A strong Board would have empowered Perot to make changes from his seat, or perhaps as CEO himself, and would not have protected the forces within the company that did not want to make changes.

Today, twenty years later, we find GM basically bankrupt. On the other hand, several bloggers and columnists have recently suggested that Perot be made the Car Czar to oversee the failing auto industry. I would say he's had the last laugh.

3. An aging business model lacking a level of investment in product innovation and technology sufficient to keep the business current with market conditions. Along these same lines, the company is trapped in an aging industry being rendered obsolete by advances in technology or new competition. The list of companies that have failed because of a decrepit business model could go on for miles. These are some of the companies that, as we said in Chapter One, cover the battlefield of dead or dying, once-great American companies. In fact, whole industries are failing because the models/products that once served them well are no longer viable. These include newspapers, airlines, the travel industry and—of course—the auto industry.

On the other hand, there are examples of industries that have invested in innovation and technology and developed new business models that are revitalizing growth within the industry. The publishing industry is one, as you'll see in the following example. (Unfortunately, as recent turmoil in the industry has shown, self-inflicted wounds by management continue to plague this industry as well.)

Reading the Signs of a Changing Marketplace

In his 2006 bestseller *The Long Tail,* Chris Anderson points to the positive example of an industry that has been able to take advantage of new technologies and trends, breathing life into a previously mature industry with limited growth potential.

The following is an excerpt from the 2004 *Wired* article, of the same name, that predated Anderson's book. He subsequently expanded the article to book-length.

"In 1988, a British mountain climber named Joe Simpson wrote a book called *Touching the Void,* a harrowing account of near death in the Peruvian Andes. It got good reviews but, after only a modest success, it was soon forgotten. Then, a decade later, a strange thing happened. Jon Krakauer wrote *Into Thin Air,* another book about a mountain-climbing tragedy, which became a publishing sensation. Suddenly, *Touching the Void* started to sell again.

"Random House rushed out a new edition to keep up with demand. Booksellers began to promote it next to their *Into Thin Air* displays, and sales rose further. A revised paperback edition, which came out in January, spent fourteen weeks on the *New York Times* Best Seller List. That same month, IFC Films released a docudrama of the story to critical acclaim. Now, *Touching the Void* outsells *Into Thin Air* more than two-to-one.

"What happened? In short, Amazon.com recommendations. The online bookseller's software noted patterns in buying behavior and suggested that readers who liked *Into Thin Air* would also like *Touching the Void.* People took the suggestion, agreed wholeheartedly, wrote rhapsodic reviews. More sales, more algorithm-fueled recommendations, and the positive feedback loop kicked in. ...

"... This is not just a virtue of online booksellers; it is an example of an entirely new economic model for the media and entertainment industries, one that is just beginning to show its power. Unlimited selection is revealing truths about what consumers want and how they want to get it in service after service, from DVDs at Netflix to music videos on Yahoo! ... People are going deep into the catalog, down the long, long list of available titles, far past what's available at Blockbuster Video, Tower Records, and Barnes & Noble. And the more they find, the more they like. As they wander further from the beaten path, they discover their taste is not as mainstream as they thought (or as they had been led to believe by marketing, a lack of alternatives, and a hit-driven culture)."

4. Over-complicating the business and profit model. Simply put, management is failing to maintain the proper cost-relationship between a single dollar of sales and the required cash profit on that dollar of sales. I refer to this as over-complicating the business and profit model and forgetting why the company is in business.

5. Poor compensation strategy for the management team, enabling unearned bonuses on a short-term basis. As any behavioral psychologist will tell you, altering the normal relationship between results and reward—in other words, rewarding poor results—can only breed incompetence and poor decision making. This condition is also the beginning of a culture of non-accountability in the entire organization. When the executive management team no longer understands the proper relationship between results and rewards, it does not pass down a sense of urgency and accountability to the body politic of the company. The end result is a culture that avoids accountability and embraces excuses. The Compensation Committee of the Board of Directors must keep the relationship between results and rewards intact or retire managers who have become too rich and lost an understanding and appreciation of the relationship between performance results and financial rewards.

Now let's move on to the strategic root causes of a TUC.

The Traditional Strategic Root Causes of a TUC

Any one of these tactical root causes—or all of them—can eventually be traced back, directly or indirectly, to bad strategic decisions, usually made years before these tactical decisions.

The most common of these strategic root causes are:

1. Failures of Vision. In this case, Boards and management teams of TUCs have not expanded their imaginations to include scenarios beyond the narrow bank of activity that falls within their comfort zones. There are numerous reasons for this, ranging from complacency and laziness to lack of funds to build or acquire new capabilities. Some good examples of TUCs that missed the "vision thing" are the big airlines like Pan American, Eastern and TWA. They were so comfortable with their niche and business models that they became lazy and failed to construct a vision broad enough to include the effects of deregulation and the emergence of a low-cost niche within their markets and new low-cost carriers like Southwest. The result? Several TUCs and bankruptcies.

2. A Wrong-headed Strategy or No Strategy. This is consistent with loss of vision but goes a step further—it is characterized by the bad strategic decision making that accompanies loss of vision. For example, a company may have failed to expand its vision to accommodate future changes in the market or technology. That, in itself, is a mistake, but the company can survive a long time if it executes an efficient business model and continues to make money. Unfortunately, as the vision blurs, bad strategic decisions are made that begin to water down the business model as the company tries to over-compensate for market forces beyond its control. Examples of the poor strategic decisions that often create TUCs in this scenario are bad acquisitions, wasted product development and R&D expenditures, wasted expenditures on regional and global expansion, and recruitment of the wrong executive talent.

There are numerous examples of TUCs that forgot or lost their vision or business models, but the one I like most really encompasses a whole industry—marketing research (MR) companies. The vision across this $25 billion industry has been exactly the same for the last twenty years: to provide the global Fortune 1,000 companies with data and research that will help their marketing departments

> As the vision blurs, bad strategic decisions are made that begin to water down the business model.

sell more products and services. The management teams of these MR firms have been very comfortable in their niche, while their value propositions to the Fortune 1,000 have deteriorated. As a result, they have gradually made bad decisions that have chipped away at a once-profitable business model.

An example of a bad decision in the MR industry is the move to lower the cost of data acquisition for market research products in an attempt to preserve profitability. This data is the raw material of their market research products and as the old adage says, "garbage in and garbage out." By lowering the cost of data, they are decreasing the value of their products, inevitably eroding their business models. I believe they have decided to lower the cost and cheapen the data because the bigger vision for their businesses escapes them.

3. Failure to Understand the Company's Business Life Cycle. The final, common strategic mistake is the Board's failure to match the skill set of the CEO and management team with the specific stage of the business life cycle that the company is entering.

The life cycles, with a description of the **right** CEO for each stage, are:

Cycle One: Seed, Start-up	Entrepreneurial CEO
Cycle Two: Continuous Improvement, Growth	Entrepreneurial CEO with strong operating skills
Cycle Three: Rapid Expansion	Operating CEO with strong sales and marketing skills
Cycle Four: Maturity and Reinvestment	Operating CEO with strong innovation skills
Cycle Five: Maturity and Exit	Experienced executive with M&A skills

Failure to match the skills of the CEO and executive team with the unique requirements of each stage will almost certainly result in some degree of serious performance failure and could turn the company into a TUC. In his book, *Great People Decisions,* Claudio Fernandez Araoz, a partner and member of the global executive committee of the leading executive search firm Egon Zehnder, addresses the issue of bad leadership decisions. He writes, "Based on the many executive searches and management appraisals I have participated in, as well as the tens of thousands of managers and executives I have met and worked with, I have no doubt about the most important reason for major company failure: bad people decisions at the top. Putting the wrong people into key positions leads to corporate failure, which leads in turn to more individual failures. One bad decision (or two or three) precipitates many more in a cascade of failure."

Admittedly, this is a very difficult match to make and Boards usually spend millions of dollars on executive recruiters and consultants to hire someone with the right stuff. But, in my experience, both the recruiters and the Boards often miss the unique and specific nature of the challenge within the life cycle.

Failure to match the skills of the CEO and executive team with the unique requirements of each stage will almost certainly result in some degree of serious performance failure.

A Classic Mismatch

One of my favorite examples of a well-intentioned miss when matching CEOs to corporate life cycles was at AT&T in the 1990s. In the late 1980s, the Justice Department broke up AT&T and forced it to sell its local phone company network and business. In my opinion, this single act served to accelerate the movement of AT&T through its normal life-cycle evolution to maturity. Since an exit was not possible, AT&T should have essentially reinvented itself and gone back to a Stage One: Start Up/Entrepreneurial model, building new products and creating a new vision. Instead, the Board tried to reconstitute itself through an M&A strategy focused on the cable industry. Accordingly, it hired a proven operator and executive familiar with M&A, Michael Armstrong. Armstrong was a proven executive with IBM and Hughes, but I argue he didn't have the right stuff for AT&T at that stage.

The proof is that AT&T today has rebounded as a company and is reaping the rewards of eventually reinventing itself, under the leadership of Ed Whitacre, as a communications and networking company built on the launch of new entrepreneurial products like Voice Tone, Internet Protect, Voice over Internet Protocol services and numerous other wireless and broadband products. The difference between Armstrong and Whitacre was the latter's deep, domain knowledge of the communications industry and his ability to translate that knowledge into an innovative entrepreneurial vision for AT&T. The same case can be made for what Steve Jobs has done for Apple, vs. his predecessors.

In closing, following the trail of current tactical root causes for a TUC back to the strategic decision-making mistakes of the past is a surefire way to understand the true problems underlying the TUC. This is what works, and I bet my reputation on it every time I take on a new TUC assignment.

4 | Selecting the Turnaround Executive and Initiating the Turnaround

According to an article in the May 2000 edition of *Harvard Business Review,* 70 percent of all corporate turnarounds fail. When you think about the definition of turnaround, it's probably not surprising so many turnarounds fail. The definition of a successful turnaround is: *A situation in which a company, which has had poor performance for an extended period, experiences a positive reversal of performance for an extended period.* Transforming an extended period of poor performance into "a positive reversal of performance for an extended period" is no easy matter. But, as my twenty-year turnaround career has shown, it's not impossible.

So why do so many turnarounds fail?

70%

of all corporate turnarounds fail.

In my opinion, 70 percent of corporate turnaround efforts fail for two distinct reasons:
- The Board of Directors and/or shareholders wait too long before initiating the turnaround effort

- The Board and/or shareholders select the wrong turnaround executive

Stuck in Neutral

Why Boards wait too long is a complex question rooted in vagaries of human behavior and the unique decision-making characteristics in a troubled company's history. However, looking in my rearview mirror, I see patterns of decision-making behavior that could explain why the Board of a troubled company does not act at the first signs of trouble.

First, the Board missed, or did not understand, the main operating and financial warning signs that the company was in trouble and an early-stage turnaround was necessary. Those signs usually include:
- At the unit-of-production level, operating profit and cash generation are starting to decline.

- Pricing is changing in the marketplace, but the company cannot respond because of a poorly documented internal pricing process and/or an undisciplined sales organization making poor and reactive daily pricing decisions.

- Customer Satisfaction (CSAT) scores are declining or not being measured properly by an independent CSAT officer. In tandem, there is a disconnect about the perception of quality between key customers and management of the company.

- There are major swings in the company cash position, not easily explained by the CEO and CFO.

- The corporate management team is fractured and managers are undermining each other, have different agendas and are working against each other or the company itself. Along this continuum of management dysfunction, bad decisions and/or no decisions are being made about the day-to-day sales, marketing, new product development, technology and operating challenges of the business. In short, the company is frozen—or worse—making bad judgment calls.

The second reason is that the Board and/or shareholders recognize the problem but choose to ignore it and truly get caught up in the classic five stages of grief. Those stages, as introduced by psychologist Elizabeth Kübler-Ross in her groundbreaking book *On Death and Dying,* are Denial, Anger, Bargaining, Depression and Acceptance. When facing what looks like the death of their enterprise, Boards and shareholders tend to immediately

If a TUC is to turn failure into success, it must have the courage to change its own destiny.

go into denial. By the time they work through the other stages of grief and finally reach acceptance, it is often too late to save the company.

However, the third and biggest reason the Board and shareholders wait too long is that they lack the courage to make a leadership change in a timely manner. If a TUC is to turn failure into success, it must have the courage to change its own destiny. That usually means turning the reins over to someone familiar with the TUC geography—a turnaround expert who can navigate around the swampland and make it to safer ground.

Changing the coach and culture of the company are courageous actions; they show that the people in charge are real custodians of shareholders' interests. Along with courage, it takes common sense, good judgment and trust to turn a TUC over to a new change agent/CEO at a time when the company is weak, failing and vulnerable. A mistake is unforgiving and could mean entering into distress, bankruptcy or even complete destruction of the company.

The Wrong Stuff

This brings us to the other major reason most turnarounds fail. When Boards do act, they frequently choose Mr. Wrong for the job. Going back to my rearview mirror, let's look at why these Boards choose Mr. Wrong.

While a company doesn't become a TUC overnight, this is certainly a situation no one plans for and few people understand. So, when a company is broken, you can't just flip through the yellow pages and call the first name under the heading "Company Repairs" as you would if the office printer broke down.

***So, it's all too easy to choose the wrong
turnaround executive. Here's why:***

Boards and/or shareholders love choosing
someone from the corporate "club" of
seasoned executives, someone who is well-
entrenched with all of the major executive
search firms and fits the physical and
experience requirements for the prototype
executive. Why do they do this? Because
it seems safe—even though it's really
not—and they cannot be criticized until
the turnaround fails. They do not truly
understand what a turnaround executive does
and the turnaround executive's skill set. I
believe that if the Board truly understood the
required skill set of a turnaround executive,
it would not make the first mistake: selecting
a perceived "safe choice." Therefore, it is
critical for the reader to understand what the
skill set of a successful turnaround executive
looks like.

> "It's not the soldiers
> who lose wars, it's
> the generals."
> Lord Wellington

The Right Stuff

Let's look at what I believe is the skill set of a
successful turnaround agent.

- **He should be a natural born leader and
  communicator.** Time and time again,
  history has shown that success—whether on
  the battlefield or in the boardroom—flows
  from the top down. As Lord Wellington
  said, "It's not the soldiers who lose wars, it's
  the generals."

Dynamic Communication in Action

Ronald Reagan was the most dynamic leader and communicator I have ever known. The things I learned about leadership from him will stay with me the rest of my life.

One lesson stands out above all others. In September 1983, while I was United States Assistant Secretary of Labor, I attended a Cabinet meeting led by Secretary of Labor Raymond J. Donovan. I was given the honor by Secretary Donovan of presenting to the President and his Cabinet the new federal training program that I had developed with the help of many dedicated civil servants and political appointees. It was a controversial piece of new legislation because it replaced the Comprehensive Employment and Training Act, known as CETA, which was a favorite political patronage program of Congress. The Job Training Partnership Act (JTPA) was one of the first public-private pieces of legislation aimed at creating partnerships to deliver services at the state and municipal levels of government, rather than through a big bureaucracy in Washington, D.C. Though standard practice today, it was radical at the time—to say the least.

The President and Cabinet loved the program because it was totally in sync with the states' rights thinking of the 1980s and the Reagan team. The question was: How would we sell the concept to the then-Democratic Congress and get it passed? Of course, being in my thirties and with an over-inflated sense of myself as a sub-Cabinet official, I was ready to take the fight to the Congress and laid my plan out to the Cabinet.

In true Reagan style, the President just shook his head and said, "Great presentation. Let's move forward, but carefully." I wondered what the "carefully" was all about.

I found out what he meant when we met after the meeting in the hall outside the Oval Office. "Al, you can get a lot more done in life if you are willing to let other people take credit for your ideas," he said, suggesting that we lead Congress to believe the program was its idea. A bell went off in my head when I realized how brilliant that approach was. I knew at that moment what got Ronald Reagan into the White House. I have used that rule as a mantra in my work as a turnaround manager and it has never failed me.

This is one way that generals win the wars: *Good thinking starts at the top and flows down through the corporate culture by allowing everyone to take ownership of good ideas.* It becomes contagious, and pretty soon good ideas are flowing all through the company and things are getting done.

- **A good turnaround executive should be a personal risk-taker with a track record to prove it.** Real leadership means being willing to take personal risks—rather than playing it safe and indulging in destructive self-interest. Unfortunately, recent years have seen a crisis of leadership in the corporate world. The media is full of stories of arrogant, self-centered CEOs whose greatest concern is the level of their own risk-free compensation packages—not the health of the companies in their charge. In fact, the problem has reached such monumental proportions that Congress felt compelled to include provisions limiting executive compensation in its October 2008 financial services bailout package.

Real leadership means standing up to the responsibility of being a fiduciary custodian for shareholders' wealth. That role—as caretaker of shareholders' interests—should be the overriding concern of a CEO; it should sit at the foundation of every decision and move he or she makes.

Greed Personified vs. Dedication and Accountability

As an American, I was embarrassed to see the three CEOs of America's auto companies, GM, Ford and Chrysler, testifying before

Congress at the end of 2008, on the heels of the Financial Services bailout hearings and one of the worst financial crises the country has ever faced. All three had their collective hands out asking the U.S. taxpayers for $25 billion to keep their essentially bankrupt businesses in operation. At the hearing, several Congressmen asked the CEOs if they would be willing to reduce their multi-million dollar salaries, give up their 2008 bonuses and turn in their private planes as conditions of the bailout loan. The room went silent and that was taken as a big NO by Congress. Is that an example of the courageous leadership and conviction required to lead a company out of trouble or, in their cases, bankruptcy? The answer to this question is a big NO!

On the other hand (and, ironically, in the same industry) a real example of courageous and unselfish leadership existed thirty years ago when Lee Iaccoca turned Chrysler around for the shareholders and the American taxpayers. Iaccoca took the reins of Chrysler in 1979 and needed a $1.5 billion bailout from U.S. taxpayers to keep Chrysler from going out of business. The automaker got the $1.5 billion, but with a number of stipulations.

In this instance, Iaccoca worked for $1 a year until the turnaround was done and promised to pay every dollar of the bailout money, with interest, back to the U.S. taxpayers—and he did just that. In addition, he assumed a very public stance behind the quality of his product, putting his personal reputation behind every K Car that came off the Chrysler assembly line. Remember TV commercials featuring him saying, "Quality is Job One"? After a public statement like that, there was no way to hide from the commitment he'd made. If he failed, he made no money and his career was ruined. But if he succeeded, he would become a legend—and that's just what happened.

The point here is that the courage to lead means that real reputation and compensation risks exist for the general leading the turnaround effort. This risk cannot be avoided, and if a leader tries to sidestep it, like the three auto CEOs, there is a high probability the turnaround effort will fail.

- **A successful turnaround agent is a maverick who knows how to run a business.** Sometimes, safeguarding shareholders' interests means having the courage to rock the corporate canoe—to navigate into unfamiliar, often turbulent waters to prevent the ship from sinking. In cases where a company is failing at core competencies—sales/marketing, customer service or technology—or advances in technology or market dynamics are rendering products obsolete, radical change may be the only route to survival.

Leading a Revolution

No one was better at rocking the corporate canoe to facilitate radical and systemic change than Jack Welsh at General Electric. In his book, *Straight from the Gut,* he describes the unpopularity of change, noting, "Change has no constituency—and a perceived revolution has even less." He wasn't afraid to face choppy seas when he took over the faltering hulk GE had become.

Knowing that he needed to change the mindset of his managers if he was to change the company in a meaningful way, Welsh, in effect, took control of the company's management development center at Crotonville, NY. He then used the management courses and seminars as forums for expressing his new rock-the-boat vision for the company and helping the company's new culture take root. Not only did he personally teach management classes during that period, but people who were around GE at the time say he really loved the role of teacher. In his book, Welsh talks about the importance of those classes, saying, "Without Crotonville, I didn't think we had a prayer. I needed to communicate the rationale for change to as big an audience as I could. Crotonville was the place to do it."

The point I like about Welsh's approach at Crotonville is the highly creative manner in which he changed the culture of GE. He realized that GE was too big to do it from his CEO's office or by traveling around the world to all of GE's facilities. So he picked the singular or *chokehold* point within the company where he could have the greatest impact—by teaching managers the new GE culture and way of doing business. Also, I think the unstated stroke of genius in Welsh's approach is that he knew himself and what he could do best to usher in change at GE—and that was to teach with a passion. Every change agent has a unique way to make change happen and every one does it with a passion.

- **Finally, a successful turnaround executive must be a true change agent with an innate ability to lead a company through the change process.** At the beginning of every turnaround, when I meet the management team and employees for the first time at an all-employee meeting, I love to tell them we are going to drive positive and productive change throughout the entire organization, from the CEO's office all the way to the mailroom. It is essential that all employees realize they are important and they are being empowered to initiate positive change from their respective roles in the company. It is because of this recognition of their value, from people at the top of the company, that new and constructive change starts. At that meeting, I like to share with employees some great observations from *In Search of Excellence* about employee empowerment—or lack thereof—in large organizations.

Children of Men

In the chapter "Productivity Through People" in their book *In Search of Excellence,* Tom Peters and Robert Waterman quote ex-Chief of Naval Operations Elmo (Bud) Zumwalt, who decried the Navy's assumption that "everyone below the rank of commander is immature." The authors point out that Zumwalt chose a different path, treating everyone as a grownup. Zumwalt recalled, "What I tried hardest to do was to ensure that every officer and man on the ship not only knew what we were about, not only why we were making each tactical evolution, however onerous, but that he also managed to understand enough about how it all fit together that he could begin to experience some of the fun and challenge that those of us in the top slots were having."

Thanks to his practices based on trust and respect, Zumwalt revolutionized the Navy in a few short years.

The authors then passed on the following poem from the General Motors auto workers' underground which speaks to Admiral Zumwalt's conclusion.

Are these men and women
Workers of the world?
or is it an overgrown nursery?
with children—gooing, slapping boys
giggling, snotty girls?
What is it about that entranceway
those gates to the plant? Is it the
guards, the showing of your badge—the smell?
Is there some invisible eye
that pierces you through and
transforms your being? Some aura
or ether, that brain and spirit washes you
and commands, "For eight hours
you shall be different."
What is it that instantaneously makes
a child out of a man?
Moments before he was a father, a husband
an owner of property, a lover, an adult.
When he spoke at least some listened
Salesmen courted his favor

Insurance men appealed to his family responsibility
and by chance the church sought his help...
But that was before he shuffled past the guard,
climbed the steps
hung his coat and
took his place along the line.

The authors note that the person who gave them the poem said he believes there is just one key to developing a "people orientation:" trust. He went on to say that only a small percentage of people will abuse that trust, but nonbelievers will offer "an infinite number of reasons why workers can't be trusted. Most organizations are governed by rules that assume the average worker is an incompetent ne'er-do-well just itching to screw up."

Isn't it amazing how similarly large organizations devalue their most valuable resource?

Let's take a deeper dive into what I believe are the characteristics of a successful change agent:

Who is the change agent?

1. A successful change agent is both a conceptualizer and an actualizer; he is capable of seeing the problem, conceptualizing a theoretical solution AND actually developing and implementing the plan for the solution. Typically, a manager is either a conceptualizer or actualizer; it's the rare corporate leader who can wield the double-edged sword. But, like a good general, a change agent must be able to devise a battle plan and then follow it to lead the troops to victory.

Of PCs and Big Macs
An example of a conceptualizer is An Wang from the old Wang Laboratories, arguably the first PC company in the world. He understood where the world of information was headed, but, when

faced with stiff competition from the likes of IBM and Hewlett-Packard, he and his son Fred failed at executing the plans to take advantage of the opportunity. The result was that Wang came to an abrupt end, while the PC industry grew and prospered and revolutionized the world.

An example of an actualizer is Ray Kroc, founder of McDonald's. The McDonald brothers, Richard and Maurice, had already invented the perfect hamburger, but it was not until they sold Ray Kroc the franchise to open ten stores that the dream could become a reality—and a MASSIVE reality at that.

As biography site Woopidoo points out: "Kroc envisioned a restaurant that ran like a factory and produced hot food, fast service, and with consistent quality no matter where he opened a restaurant. He saw food preparation as a process and broke it down into steps that could be duplicated in any of his restaurants. This way he could keep the product the same no matter where the McDonald's was located.

"Low franchise fees made it easy to open new stores but cut into any potential profits for Kroc. As a result, Kroc decided to purchase the land on which McDonald's would open and ultimately serve as a landlord. He set

Like a good general, a change agent must be able to devise a battle plan and then follow it to lead the troops to victory.

up the Franchise Realty Corporation in 1956 and was able to purchase tracks of land in order to help him produce a profit for his company. By 1960 there were over 200 McDonald's around the United States.

"Kroc saw his franchise as a way to sell a service, not food. After all, Big Boy, Dairy Queen, and A&W were already established restaurant chains. Ray Kroc needed McDonald's to stand out. Consistency was the key and he made sure that every McDonald's ran the same. He established national advertising campaigns to support his restaurants and took the brand international in 1971 to Japan and Germany."

By the time Kroc, the ultimate actualizer, died of natural causes in 1984, McDonald's was one of America's biggest companies.

2. Successful change agents always feel a powerful sense of urgency; they are driven to finish the job as quickly and efficiently as possible. This sense of urgency is necessary to re-energize the organization and reverse the negative momentum created by the business performance issues. This drive to reach the finish line prompts the best of the best to take dramatic steps—for instance, moving into a not-so-comfortable hotel room close to the company, in order to be close at hand and stay there until the job is finished.

3. The best change agent is a borderline workaholic who prides himself on working longer and harder than anyone else in the company. Boredom is usually the greatest form of stress for the change agent and, like a shark, if he is not moving he is dying. This new work ethic sets a standard for the management team and often weeds out managers who—while they may talk a good game—aren't really committed to the turnaround. I often say that a successful turnaround requires a 150 percent commitment from everyone

involved. The change agent should demonstrate what that level of commitment actually looks like.

4. The change agent should have a unique ability to make the solution to complicated situations simple. The term KISS (Keep It Simple Stupid) definitely applies to change agents. I like to say that a problem must always be solved at the lowest common denominator, where things are their simplest.

5. An artist and scientist at heart, a change agent understands the value of quality and good workmanship. Perfection is probably not the right word for a change agent. In fact, like an artist, he realizes it often takes several sketches to reach a masterpiece. But a good change agent is proud of his craft and determined to create a product that adds value in the marketplace—if not a transformative work of art, at least a solid piece of workmanship. The most successful change agents are scientists, as well as artists, who operate with well-defined models, in which the sum of the parts adds up to the right outcome, and every aspect of the process is measurable.

6. Good change agents display a willingness—even a desire—to make tough decisions, even if they negatively impact coworkers, vendors, lenders or other participants in the turnaround process. They understand clearly that, in the world of TUCs, there is no gain without pain. They know that the turnaround gods will exact payment in return for success. A perfect example of a situation requiring a tough decision is the mess facing whatever turnaround executive or change agent tackles the necessary Time Warner turnaround. He will have to make the difficult decision to sell off or decouple AOL from the parent company. This acquisition was one of the biggest M&A mistakes of all time, and Time Warner cannot be fixed without admitting the mistake and eliminating AOL from Time Warner.

The Art of the Turnaround

The process of turning a struggling company around is very much like the art and science of military battle. In *The Art of War,* the sixth-century BC masterpiece, military strategist Sun Tzu might have been describing the process of turning a troubled company around. He said that military strategy is affected by both physical and objective conditions in the environment and the subjective, changing actions of personalities acting in that environment. He taught that strategy is not planning in the sense of working through a to-do list, but rather that it requires quick and appropriate responses to changing conditions. Planning only works in a controlled environment, not in a dynamic environment like a business, where circumstances change and competing plans collide, creating unexpected situations.

7. The successful change agent is committed to wealth creation. No matter how much money he has made—personally or as the caretaker of shareholder value in other turnarounds—the good change agent is dedicated, at his very core, to shareholder wealth creation, constantly working to enrich the shareholders who have trusted him with the company's fortunes.

8. Change agents never fall in love with their work and get too close to the emotional aspects of running the business or working with the people. An exit that maximizes shareholder value may be just around the corner, so personal emotions should not prevent a change agent from implementing the exit strategy that is most beneficial to the company and its shareholders.

9. Like any professional, a good change agent can be recognized by a body of work over many years. The landscape of turnaround failures is littered with one-deal wonders who lucked out. A troubled company's leadership should never entrust its turnaround to a change agent without a clear record of successful turnarounds—any more than you

would trust an untried surgeon with complex surgery to correct a life-threatening condition. When evaluating a change agent's background, a Board should ask:

- Does the change agent have a documented and proven model or blueprint for success?
- Are shareholders or investors from the last transaction willing to invest in the current transaction undertaken by the change agent?
- Will executives from the last transaction bet their careers and future compensation on the change agent again?

10. Most of all, a good change agent is an inspirational leader who managers and rank-and-file employees in the troubled company admire—and possibly hate at the same time. The change agent shows, often for the first time, the value of a disciplined plan and the tough love required to be successful. Often, employees who quit or are terminated have so much respect for the change agent, they are willing—and anxious—to work for him in another time and place.

It's virtually impossible to overemphasize the importance of choosing a change agent with a proven track record AND a proven turnaround model. When your company is in trouble—and especially in economically turbulent times—this is your best assurance of reaching a plateau of safety and success.

In the next few chapters, we'll look in detail at the **Angrisani Hierarchy of Value Creation Model™ (AHVCM)** and how it works to turn TUCs around and maximize shareholder value.

5 | Introducing the Proven Model for Change

The battle to achieve a successful turnaround is largely fought before the turnaround ever begins. The turnaround executive must have a proven model to create the discipline required to conceptualize the turnaround plan and ultimately to actualize the plan.

In my case, the model has been constructed around years of experience and outcomes that have made it clear to me which solutions work and which do not solve the specific problems of a TUC. The model is also a way for the Board of Directors and shareholders to get a sense of what they are buying when they entrust their company to a turnaround executive and literally put the future of the company in his hands. Without a proven model, the company leadership and shareholders run the same risk a potential homeowner runs by allowing a contractor to build a new home without first agreeing on the blueprint and budget.

Toward creating the right turnaround plan for a specific company and its unique situation, I usually conduct a sixty- to ninety-day full diagnostic assessment of the TUC, at my own expense. The assessment covers all pertinent financial, operational, sales, legal and strategic drivers of the business and root causes of the problems.

Once the diagnostic is complete, I create an outline of a turnaround plan consistent with the five phases of my turnaround model, the Angrisani Hierarchy of Value Creation Model (AHVCM). I present this plan to the Board of Directors and seek general consensus on the plan before negotiating a contract to serve the company. (Believe me, when times get a little tough and results are in question during the turnaround process, the fact that all key stakeholders are on board with the plan is what keeps me, the Board of Directors and the shareholders all in the same boat and pulling together to make the turnaround a success.)

Figure 2: Angrisani Hierarchy of Value Creation Model

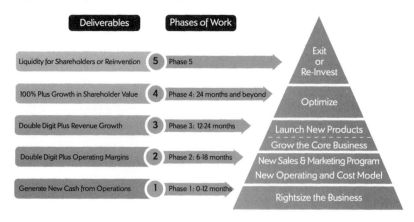

Comprehensive TUC Assessment
Here are the issues I assess when determining whether or not to undertake a turnaround process.

Financial:
- What is the operating profit (loss) for a single unit of production?
- What is the specific Cost of Goods Sold (COGS), and what are the direct labor, sales and marketing and overhead costs of the business?
- What are truly fixed vs. truly variable costs, and what will it cost to eliminate the fixed costs?
- How can I "re-silo" revenue and expense into viable profit and loss centers to further reduce cost and to better focus revenue generation?
- Within those re-siloed profit and loss centers, what are the products that are winners and losers from a profit and complexity perspective?
- What is the true cash-generation capability of the business at the unit of production level?
- What are the non-cash expenses of the business—like depreciation—and what is their life?
- What are current capital expenses (CAPEX) and can they be reduced going forward?
- What is the carrying cost of debt, and how long will it take to pay it off?
- What are hidden liabilities and investment requirements that could impact cash-generation capabilities during the turnaround?

Operational:
- How complicated is the company's production and distribution infrastructure?
- How effective is the company's technology infrastructure, including R&D and IT?
- What does it cost to produce and deliver each product based on complexity?
- What is the direct labor configuration and cost, and can it be reduced and at what cost?
- What is the real estate situation?

- What is the experience level of the operations leadership and their work ethic?
- Does the company have a satisfactory customer satisfaction or quality program and is it part of the day-to-day business?
- Does the company understand supply chain management and practice it?

Sales and Marketing:
- What is the sales model and can I bring in my customized PAMTS program without too much disruption? PAMTS is an integrated and seamless process for growing sales and revenue. It stands for Promotion, Advertising, Marketing, Telesales, Sales administered in steps and designed to eliminate friction in the ultimate sales interaction with the client. (I'll go into more detail about this program in the next chapter.)
- What is the commission plan, and can I bring in my plan without too much disruption?
- Does the company understand and have a sales recruiting pipeline?
- What is the culture of sales leadership and the sales organization? Tolerant (tolerating failure and missing sales goals) vs. bottom line?
- Does the company have a bottom-up annual sales and revenue planning system, planning from client to client?
- Does the company use Salesforce.com or a similar program to collect and control information?
- What is the relationship between U.S. vs. international sales and how is it coordinated?
- Are sales and operations working off the same page and unified in their customer facing?
- What is the experience of the sales leadership, work ethic and sense of urgency?
- Is the Marketing department strategic or tactical?
- Does Marketing understand promotion techniques?
- Does Pricing report to Marketing, Sales or Finance?

Overhead in general:

- How capable are the CFO, Finance team and the financial and information management systems they work with?
- How fat is the remainder of the personnel overhead infrastructure?
- Does the company have a good Human Resources director and documented compensation plans?
- Is the bonus plan performance-driven vs. MBO-based (Management by Objective), and can it be changed without amending plans? How effective and expensive is the IT infrastructure?
- What is the legal situation, and are there current or hidden lawsuits that can change the outcome of the turnaround?
- Can I reduce overhead to between 10 to 15 percent of every dollar of revenue?
- What are the consultant and vendor outside contractor situations and can I reduce that expense?
- Can I move overhead or any form of production offshore and lower costs?

Strategic:

- What is the competition situation?
- What is the product and business obsolescence situation?
- What is the new technology and overall business threat situation?
- What is the merger and acquisition opportunity?
- Can we create new products and roll them out to create new revenue?
- Are there any hidden new products in the current product suite that we can carve out and grow through investment?

Borrowing from the Art and Science of Psychology

If you search the database of your mind back to Psychology 101, you'll recall humanistic psychologist Abraham Maslow's Hierarchy of Needs. You will often see Maslow's Hierarchy of Needs represented as a pyramid with five levels. The first four levels of the pyramid are what Maslow terms the Deficiency levels—and with good reason. These are basic needs, beginning with physiological needs like food, health and shelter, moving up to friendship and intimacy, and finally on to the need for self-esteem and confidence. If these needs aren't met, an individual is left with a feeling that something basic is missing in life—a sense of deficiency. Only after these needs are met can someone move on to the Growth needs under the general heading of Self-actualization.

Figure 3: Maslow's Hierarchy of Needs

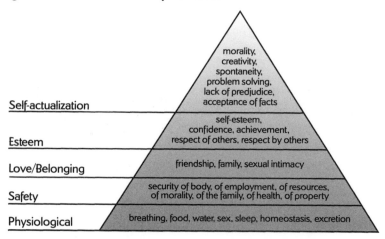

It makes perfect sense to borrow from Maslow's model because businesses—like humans—are living, breathing organisms with distinct needs and vulnerabilities. If you doubt this, you've never worked in a sick business and watched how quickly distress and anxiety can spread when basic needs aren't met.

Like Maslow's model, AHVCM is a pyramid with steps to ensure a troubled company's basic survival at its foundation. Once those needs—beginning with rightsizing the business and moving on through building the core business and launching new products—are met, we can work to optimize performance and, finally at the apex of the pyramid, implement a strategy for putting control back in the hands of the management team and Board and promoting shareholder wealth creation.

Businesses — like humans — are living, breathing organisms with distinct needs and vulnerabilities.

Before I get into some detail about the five phases of the model in the next chapter, let me point out that *the model and turnaround plan constitute the science of the process, which must be accompanied by the art for the plan to succeed. Simply put, the art refers to my ability to apply the pieces of the model and the turnaround plan in a slightly different way for each turnaround, to meet each company's specific needs. Although the phases, or building blocks, of the model are always the same, the manner—and sometimes the timing—of how they are applied to the problem at hand can be different.*

For example, in one of my early turnarounds, the company had double-digit annual growth, but its business model, profit model and cost model were broken. In short, the more it sold, the more money it lost. In this situation, I rightsized the company (Phase One) and reconstituted the operating and cost model (first half of Phase Two) at the same time. Once this was accomplished, I proceeded directly to Optimization (Phase Four) and then quickly exited the business through a merger.

Most TUCs have lost their ability to create new shareholder value in public or private markets.

In another turnaround situation, the opposite was the case. The business, profit and cost models were very efficient, but the company was losing money because it needed more sales volume. In this situation I skipped all of Phase One and Phase Two and started at Phase Three, developing new products and initiating actions to grow revenue. Fortunately, the combination of a few new, well-thought-out products and my PAMTS program produced a meaningful growth in revenue and profits and a major increase in the public stock price of the company.

Laying the Groundwork for the Model

Reconceptualizing the Core Business

As a means of laying the groundwork for the model, *I preface the process by reconceptualizing (reinventing) the core business of the company to make it relevant again from the perspective of driving new shareholder value.* Most TUCs have lost their ability—or at least their belief in their ability—to create new shareholder value in public or private markets. Typically, the stakeholders—the Board of Directors, shareholders and management team—are too close to the forest to see the obsolescence that has slithered into their business. In fact, they are usually on auto pilot, doing the same things over and over—the very things that have put their business in peril. At some point in the early part of the process, I like to ask the management team to read the humorous, but eye-opening, historical account in the following sidebar. It's a great illustration of why it is essential for a TUC to think out of the box and creatively reconceptualize the business.

The reconceptualization is usually nothing short of reinventing the business, using core competencies and infrastructures that currently exist. It's important to point out that it does not mean starting all over again from scratch. Think of a reconceptualization as a redesign and build-out of an old house. It needs to be both gutted and expanded, but you don't need to dig a new foundation or change the core support infrastructure of the building. In order to adequately reconceptualize a business model, the turnaround executive must have:

- The creativity to see the new design of the business model
- The experience to understand how to mix the best of the old model with elements of the new, like new technologies and products

As the following examples shows, businesses and whole civilizations are very resistant to change.

Railroad Tracks
(Be sure to read through to the end of this tale, and you'll be rewarded with a great twist.)

The U.S. standard railroad gauge (distance between the rails) is four feet, eight and one-half inches. That's an exceedingly odd number.

Why was that gauge used? Because that's the way they built them in England, and English expatriates built the U.S. railroads.

Why did the English build them like that? Because the first rail lines were built by the same people who built the pre-railroad tramways, and that's the gauge they used.

Why did they use that gauge then? Because the people who built the tramways used the same jigs and tools they used for building wagons, which used that wheel spacing.

Why did the wagons have that particular odd wheel spacing? Well, if they tried to use any other spacing the wagon wheels would break on some of the old, long-distance roads in England, because that's the spacing of the wheel ruts.

So who built those old rutted roads? Imperial Rome built the first long-distance roads in Europe (including those in England) for their legions. The roads have been used ever since.

And the ruts in the roads? Roman war chariots formed the initial ruts, which everyone else had to match for fear of destroying their wagon wheels if they didn't. Because the chariots were made for Imperial Rome, they were alike in the matter of wheel spacing.

So the United States standard railroad gauge of four feet, eight and one-half inches is derived from the original specifications for an Imperial Roman war chariot. Bureaucracies live forever.

So, the next time someone hands you a specification/procedure/process and you wonder, "What horse's ass came up with this?" you may be exactly right. Imperial Roman army chariots were made just wide enough to accommodate the rear ends of two war horses.

Now, the twist to the story:

When you see a space shuttle sitting on its launch pad, there are two booster rockets attached to the sides of the main fuel tank.

These are solid rocket boosters, or SRBs. The SRBs are made by Thiokol at its factory in Utah. The engineers who designed the SRBs would have preferred to make them a bit fatter, but the SRBs had to be shipped by train from the factory to the launch site. Clearly, the SRBs could be no wider than the train tracks on which they would travel.

As in the great pyramids of Ancient Egypt, the sequencing must be precisely by-design or the structure will not stand.

So, a major design feature of what is arguably the most advanced transportation system in the world was determined almost two thousand years ago by the width of a horse's ass.

The moral of the story? Don't let horses' asses control your company; don't be afraid of change and think out of the box!

Once I have worked through reconceptualization in some detail (but before it is 100 percent complete), I move on to constructing the details of the five phases of work in the turnaround. The detail for these five phases usually takes the form of a list of specific tasks to be undertaken and the timeline for completion. I purposely avoid developing extensive narrative around the tasks in each phase; narrative can become a form of rationalization, and I prefer to focus on a call for action. Specific tasks, with specific deliverable dates, keep me focused, sharp and accountable—first to myself, then to the plan. If I miss a deadline, it's no one's fault but my own, because the deadline was clearly and simply stated in the plan I created.

Every one of the stated tasks has a great sense of urgency because the next task or building block can't be put in place until the current task or building block I'm working on is completed. As you can see in the graphic of the model (Figure 2), each phase of work—with its embedded tasks—is like one big block in the pyramid, with the foundation being laid for the next phase of work. As in the great pyramids of Ancient Egypt, the sequencing must be precisely by-design or the structure will not stand.

These phases and building blocks, sequenced in the proper order and supporting subsequent tasks and phases, are what create shareholder wealth. As the process progresses, each higher phase of work activity creates increasing value for the company that is being turned around or reinvented and expanded via reconceptualization. By following the sequencing and hierarchy of value creation in the model, we create companies that are greater than the sum of their parts—proving once again that one and one sometimes equals three.

In the following chapters I'll show you, in detail, how the phases of AHVCM work to rebuild troubled companies—when the process is in the right hands.

The Proven
Turnaround Model

6 | Rightsize and Redesign the Business

When undertaken by the right change agent, and in the proper sequence, *the phases of AHVCM work together to revitalize and modernize a TUC and, when the process is complete, maximize shareholder value.* As I said in the last chapter, this precise application of the process should be blended with artful modification—based on a company's individual needs. So you'll note that timelines and parameters of various tasks are fluid—based on how quickly and completely a particular company reacts to the strong medicine in each phase. (It's important to note that timelines between various phases sometimes overlap; because of the urgency that marks every turnaround, it makes sense to begin work on a succeeding phase as soon as the phase-in-progress is proving successful.)

Phase One: Rightsizing the Business

Figure 4

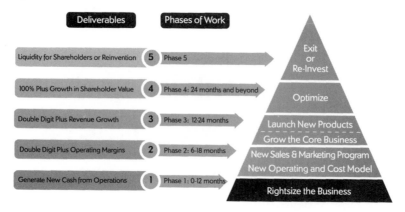

Timeline: Completed within first ninety days and fine-tuned during first year.

MSN's Encarta online dictionary defines rightsizing as: Bringing something to appropriate size; bringing a company to what is considered to be its *optimal* size, sometimes by reducing a workforce.

Rightsizing is a critical, foundational first step in optimizing a company's performance and inevitably maximizing shareholder value.

The goal of the rightsizing effort is to make cash flow positive, or to generate additional cash flow from operations, as a means of creating positive momentum and cash fuel for the turnaround. ***Remember this statement: Turnarounds are all about creating more cash.*** Rightsizing is the first of many actions to drive more and more cash from operations.

The following is the step-by-step process I follow to rightsize a TUC:

Turnarounds are all about creating more cash.

- First, I focus on substantial Earnings Before Interest, Tax, Depreciation and Amortization (EBITDA) growth as the objective of the rightsizing. In service companies that I have managed, the desired EBITDA target after the turnaround is at least 20 percent of revenues. The rightsizing is the first step toward achieving this objective.

- The next step is to assign specific expense targets, as a percentage of revenue, to all other expense categories, including gross margin, direct labor, sales and marketing, and general and administrative (G&A). The objective of assigning these expenses is to ensure that the rightsizing touches all major expense groups and establishes a culture of expense accountability in the company.

- Then, I reconstruct the overall Profit and Loss (P&L) statement into no fewer than three, and no more that five, sub P&Ls that best reflect entrepreneurial business units within the overall company. In short, I break the company up, on paper, into sub-business units, each of which is a reflection of how the company may have looked when it was growing and successful.

- Within each of those groups, I do bottom-up rightsizing, matching expenses with revenues. In each case, I insist on a 20 percent EBITDA margin.

- Next, I incorporate those expense cuts from the five P&Ls into the corporate rightsizing effort. This ensures that unproductive expenses are eliminated but does not put revenue at risk.

- Corporate overhead expenses that cannot be assigned to the individual P&Ls should be identified and trimmed. P&L managers make the decisions about what to keep and what to eliminate, based on the value each service brings to the group. The remaining corporate expenses should not be brought back into the individual P&Ls. Instead, it should be re-evaluated every six months by the P&L managers and trimmed accordingly.

- Finally, going forward with the next elements of the rightsizing, which include terminations, appointment of new leadership and reporting responsibilities, we use the template of the newly created sub-business groups to drive actions from the bottom-up.

Phase Two
Part One: Redesign of Sales and Marketing

Figure 5

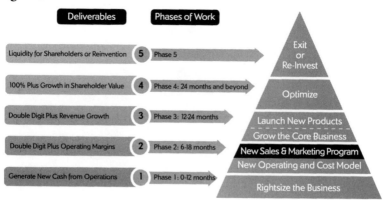

Timeline: Initiate after rightsizing is underway and to be completed within twelve months of initiation.

The goal of Sales and Marketing redesign is to create a more purposeful, efficient and integrated approach to making profitable sales. My theory is that if a sale cannot be made with an appropriate profit margin, it should not be made at all. All too often, TUCs' sales organizations are "selling against the house," making their commissions, but selling products and/or services at such low prices that shareholders are being denied appropriate profits on each dollar's worth of sales. If optimal shareholder value is our ultimate goal, it's clear that this practice has to be stopped immediately.

> If a sale cannot be made with an appropriate profit margin, it should not be made at all.

To be sure that every dollar of sales has an appropriate margin, the sales organization must be redesigned to make *the sale the last stop along the train of an integrated selling process that I call PAMTS™*, which I referenced in Chapter 5. My proprietary PAMTS process stands for, in order of execution:

1. Promotion
2. Advertising
3. Marketing
4. Telesales
5. Sales

In order to make each dollar of sales yield higher profit, a chain of activities that precedes the sales process must be well thought out and integrated. This allows the salesperson to sell downhill with less marketplace resistance and sufficient leverage in the marketplace to hold

The pressure to cut
prices is intense. My
advice: DON'T DO IT.

pricing targets and profit margins on each
dollar of sales.

*Let me briefly discuss each of the elements of
the PAMTS process:*

Promotion: This is a process of tactically
promoting products, based on targeted
campaigns designed to work in concert with
supply and demand for product inventory.
Excess inventory is wasted cash; it serves no
purpose sitting on a shelf. (This is an especially
big problem for a cash-hungry TUC.)

Promotion is a way to energize the demand
for a product and to selectively lower prices
without across-the-board changes in pricing
policy. At the outset of every turnaround,
the pressure to cut prices is intense. *My
advice: DON'T DO IT. Across-the-board
price reductions are public recognition of
a devaluation of the business itself and
are only appropriate in a liquidation
environment.* Instead, promotion of
select products is a way to make required
adjustments to market conditions and raise
cash from stagnant inventory.

Advertising: Advertising for the sake of
advertising in TUCs is an absolute waste of
cash. In fact, in TUCs the advertising budget
should be eliminated in the rightsizing. Then, a
more efficient and targeted advertising budget
should be built from a zero base, specifically

around the Promotion strategy just discussed. This will ensure that advertising cost is a variable cost of each dollar of sales.

Marketing: In TUCs, the only marketing that is relevant is tactical marketing. The marketing effort in a TUC should be focused on the "how-to" aspects of promotion, advertising, telesales and sales support. The "how-to" should encompass activities like rollout plans, competitive information, mystery shopping and advertising materials.

A TUC should refrain from strategic rethinking of markets, products and competition at this point. These macro activities often confuse the turnaround effort and its goal: to produce cash and profits, and refocus and re-energize the company.

Telesales: Telesales is the most efficient way to sell in a TUC and should be used, whenever possible, in place of the traditional sales effort, or as a setup for traditional sales activity. Most TUCs have wasteful sales budgets and activity rife with inefficiency. Telesales activities have lower commission structures and more efficient sales delivery infrastructure. They are a great tool for shaking up the sales force and driving toward more efficient sales activity.

Sales: The PAMT portion of the PAMTS process, if conducted correctly, is like a springboard under good salespeople, whose feet are on the street building relationships and closing sales. PAMT properly conditions the sales environment, making sure sales efforts will be more efficient, as evidenced by:
- Higher conversion rates
- Stable and high margins on sales
- Less turnover in the sales force
- Better understanding of the company value and pricing proposition in the marketplace
- Stronger client relationships

The rule of thumb is to have a pipeline that can replace 10 percent of the sales force at any one time.

After PAMTS has been installed and is operating well, several other changes need to be made to redesign the sales and marketing program.

Now is the time to hire a dedicated, internal recruiter of sales talent to create a pipeline of new talent to replace the portion of the sales staff certain to fail in the new structure, with its focus on accountability.

The rule of thumb is to have a pipeline that can replace 10 percent of the sales force at any one time.

It's also important to change the sales commission program to ensure that the commission clock starts anew each quarter. Commission payouts should reflect the cumulative performance of the salesperson year-to-date, and payouts shouldn't start until at least 90 percent of the quarterly goal has been achieved and target gross margins are achieved. Most sales commission programs in TUCs are too liberal. As businesses fail and there is less oversight across the board, structure and accountability virtually disappear from commission programs. In fact, TUCs' sales forces become de facto "loss leaders," with salespeople selling against the house and making commissions against goals that are not consistent with the company's profit objectives.

To more closely control sales and marketing costs following institution of a PAMTS program, I take these steps:

- Make sure that sales and marketing or PAMTS expenses do not exceed 12 to 15 percent of every revenue dollar.

- Fire the bottom 10 percent of producers, even if they are achieving sales targets. This keeps everyone honest and ensures that selling does not stop when sales goals are achieved. I replace these people with less expensive and hungrier employees who have come through the sales recruitment pipeline.

- Carefully monitor travel and entertainment expenses for sales personnel and cut back funding for individual sales representatives who aren't achieving goals.

- Establish a pricing function independent of the sales team, which measures pricing performance for consistency and efficiency on a daily basis. I like to initiate a pricing customer satisfaction measurement tool in order to determine the quality of each pricing proposal issued by the company. This new pricing function should report to Finance, with a dotted line to Sales management. Finance then uses pricing as an element in its overall measure of the effectiveness of turnaround efforts to drive profits and EBITDA. Marketing and sales are often dismayed by efforts to reduce their control over pricing; they see pricing as a tool they can use to drive sales. But remember this: The value of a product is not what you can sell it for, but how much profit you can make by selling it. If you can't make sufficient profit for the shareholders from a particular product, you should find a product that will earn the desired margin.

- Quickly implement an integrated sales platform like Salesforce.com so all sales personnel can share customer and account information in real time. The success of tactical sales and overall PAMTS strategy depends on information being readily available—at all times.

- Finally—and quietly—I start looking for the winners and losers in the product suite and start feeding the winners and starving the losers, from a PAMTS process perspective. By the end of the turnaround, 10 to 20 percent of existing product revenue will be eliminated or shut down and replaced with new products and revenues. (This is something I'll discuss further in Phase Three.)

A final, critical note about sales and marketing: *Never be afraid to replace the Sales and Marketing management team if they're not true believers in this redesign of your sales and marketing program. In this critical time in your company, leaders are either apostles for change or obstacles on the road to recovery.*

Part Two: Redesigning the Operations and Cost Model

Figure 6

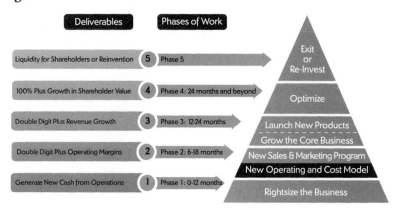

Timeline: Start after rightsizing is initiated and conclude after making company the high-quality, low-cost provider of service in the industry.

By the time I arrive on the scene at a TUC, the company's operating model and product delivery infrastructure are badly broken, with costs out of control. The operations function is like the assembly line of the company, and without an efficient assembly line, the factory shuts down. So Job One is usually to fix the factory.

Fixing the Factory

The first task is to identify inefficiencies in various components of the service delivery process—including work flow, staffing, plant locations and technology and IT infrastructure—and to redesign the factory to eliminate these inefficiencies. This is best accomplished by taking the redesign out of the hands of the operations team, and instead constructing a cross-company working group to redesign the factory and oversee the building of a more efficient operations platform. One of the hardest decisions this group will have to make is to identify and terminate what I like to call bad revenue, or revenue that cannot be efficiently processed through the operations infrastructure because of highly customized work requirements. This is usually low- or no-margin work that healthy competitors wisely shun, but that the TUC's sales team takes on in order to create the illusion—and it is an illusion—of sales performance. This work makes the problem of fixing the factory more complex and should be eliminated at the outset of the fix-the-factory effort.

Parallel to fixing the factory should be an effort by the IT and R&D teams to use technology and automation to eliminate as much direct labor as possible in operations. This is best accomplished by initiating some healthy competition between IT and operations management, asking each to suggest ways to reduce headcount and direct labor expenses. But remember that, in the end, technology is your friend when it comes to reducing operations costs. A TUC's long-term approach should be to make strategic IT investments that help reduce addiction to high-cost labor.

At this time, it is also critical to install a supply chain management team to focus intensely on reducing COGS and improving gross margin. In my experience, this has always been one of the greatest areas of savings in a TUC and it is surprisingly easy to accomplish. The supply chain team can make a big difference by centralizing purchasing, installing daily controls and leveraging every purchasing decision into a less expensive acquisition of the raw materials for the business. In a TUC, there is usually little or no purchasing discipline, so the supply chain team can make a huge impact.

At this stage, it's also critical that the customer's voice is heard. So I install a strong Customer Satisfaction (CSAT) measurement tool to serve as a barometer of customer pleasure (or, in the case of TUCs, usually lack thereof). There is no better forecaster of future sales than a CSAT; it's better than sales backlog, sales calls and so on. In fact, I believe that the foundation for any successful business is a quality product or service delivered in a highly efficient manner. For example, IBM teaches its sales executives that 50 percent of future sales are based on the delivery of quality service to clients today.

Hopefully, as we continue the process of redesigning the operations and cost model, an increasing number of customers will view the TUC as the high-quality/low-cost leader in the market space. And that is the truest measure of success.

7 | Grow and Optimize the Business

Once we've completed the Rightsizing and Redesign phases of the turnaround model, it's time to move on to grow the core business, launch new products and optimize operations. This is the stage where a TUC is truly transformed into a successful, high-performing business.

When a TUC's core business is growing again, there's an unmistakable energy driving the business through the rest of the turnaround.

Phase Three

Part One: Grow the Core Business

Figure 7

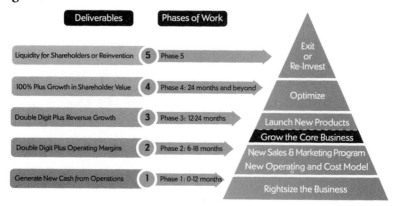

Timeline: Initiate as soon as operating and cost model redesign are underway and new sales and marketing programs are in place.

Sine Qua Non

A TUC will not turn around on a sustainable basis unless and until its core business is organically growing again. The Latin expression sine qua non, "without this, nothing," applies perfectly to the task of successfully turning around a TUC. Every one of the Phases of Work in the turnaround model can be executed perfectly, but without the eventual ability to grow the core business, a TUC will not turn around on a long-term basis.

So, when I initially analyze a TUC, I must feel—absolutely—that long-term growth of the core business can be sustained. I must feel confident that I can achieve a minimum of between 8 to 12 percent steady annual growth of the core business, with acceptable profit margins as dictated by the business model. Here's why: The ultimate goal of revenue growth in a TUC is the steady generation of, first, cash and, second, EBITDA. Slow growth with high profits or high growth with low or no profits does not produce the steady and dependable flow of cash into the company treasury to fuel all of the other elements and phases of work required in the turnaround effort.

> A TUC will not turn around on a sustainable basis unless and until its core business is organically growing again.

So how do we grow the core business in a TUC, which is likely to be losing revenues and profits when I walk in the door? If there were a simple answer to this, more turnarounds would succeed. That is why many turnaround executives position themselves to Boards as gunslingers who ride into Dodge and save the day by cost-cutting alone. This is a romantic idea, but a good way to find Dodge Hill—the famous gunfighters graveyard.

No self-respecting turnaround book can ignore the lessons of Chain Saw Al (Al Dunlap), perhaps the original turnaround gunslinger, who thought cutting costs was the means to the end of a successful turnaround. Just look at what he did at Sunbeam Corporation in the late 1990s and the lessons are clear. First, he axed one-half of the company's twelve thousand employees, as well as numerous other operating and overhead expenses. Then, when the company did not turn, he made the classic mistake of trying to buy revenue growth with an M&A strategy that cost Sunbeam $2.5 billion that it should never have spent. (What was the Board thinking? Where were

I make it perfectly clear
to employees that Sales
are Job One.

the checks and balances?) These acquisitions included name-brand companies like First Alert, Inc., Signature USA, Inc. and Coleman Co., but they weren't the right additions to create needed revenue growth at Sunbeam.

This Al's philosophy is that cutting costs and rightsizing the business are only half the battle—and maybe the least important half. A successful turnaround MUST include organic growth of the core business or the turnaround will fail.

Cost-cutting alone cannot save the TUC. But cost-cutting to rightsize the cost and profit model, combined with the steady growth of quality revenues, or revenues with appropriate margins in the core business, is what wins the gunfight. This is the formula for a successful turnaround.

So how do you grow the core business of a TUC?

The first step in the process is for the turnaround executive to take a high-profile role in the fight to build long-term revenue growth. I make it perfectly clear to employees that Sales are Job One. I borrowed this angle from Lee Iacocca who, when he turned around Chrysler, told the employees that Quality was Job One. *He picked the most important variable in his process and aligned his own future success or failure with it.*

I follow Iacocca's lead but take a more extreme approach to be sure I get my message across. I tell the troops that we are locked in a righteous struggle for survival and that they will carry me out on my shield from the battlefield—like any good general—or we will succeed. I then assume temporary leadership of the growth phase of the business (in effect, taking control of the sales program), which is tantamount to putting myself at the point of the charge or attack. Inevitably, the troops rally behind that commitment and start believing that we can again succeed at selling; they realize they are not in the struggle alone.

Cost-cutting alone cannot save the TUC.

At this point, I like to close the deal by telling them that we can be a world-class sales organization and ask them to read Seth Godin's little book called *The Dip,* and to focus on his:

Seven Reasons You Might Fail to Become The Best in the World
1. You run out of time (and quit).
2. You run out of money (and quit).
3. You get scared (and quit).
4. You're not serious about it (and quit).
5. You lose interest or enthusiasm or settle for being mediocre (and quit).
6. You focus on the short term instead of the long term (and quit when the short term gets too hard).
7. You pick the wrong thing at which to be the best in the world (and quit).

Even clients who have
turned to competitors
want you to succeed.

Critical Allies in the Struggle

Once I am in control of Sales, I set up client meetings with the Sales leadership team and we re-enlist clients, many of whom have already left the fold. My experience has been that even clients who have turned to competitors want you to succeed and will give you a second and third chance if you are sincere, fix the problems and ask for their help. I make it clear to any major client that he can call me at any time. This kind of access—100 percent of the time— sends a message of absolute accountability to the organization; problems can no longer be swept under the rug of the "I-scratch-your-back-you-scratch-mine" culture of a TUC.

I then turn up the heat under the sales team and send daily performance stats, held up against plans, to all company offices, so all representatives and sales managers can see how each representative stacks up. The document is color-coded and easy to understand: Green means a representative is ahead of plan, black means he is on-plan, and red is a great predictor of a pink slip next quarter, unless a representative can move into black or green territory. This system—a big step forward toward accountability—allows us to demonstrate clear objectivity in termination decisions. This is especially important when it's necessary to terminate popular, but inefficient, sales managers and personnel.

And, as an accompaniment to the new commission structure discussed in Phase Two, I use an old but very effective technique—sales contests—to drive higher levels of performance and efficiency.

As soon as a new sense of sales energy, accountability and performance emerges, I am quick to appoint a sales manager—someone who has most enthusiastically and efficiently embraced the example that I set while driving the sales program.

At this point of transition, I very quickly turn my attention to organizing a new product development effort, to begin the process of finding new—but compatible—products that can be sold through the renewed sales distribution organization.

Part Two: Launch New Products

Figure 8

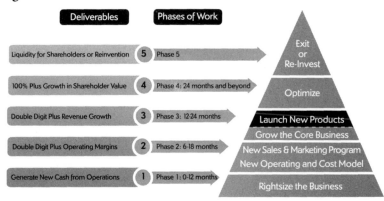

Timeline: Undertake the launch of new products as soon as the leadership of the renewed sales effort has been transitioned from working with me to the new sales manager.

The goal of the new product development phase of work is to generate a stream of new, but related, products that can re-energize the sales effort and leverage the sales infrastructure by putting more products to sell in the sales kits of the representatives. Also, by broadening the product and revenue base, downside protection is created for the inevitability that some older products will not survive the turnaround process.

The best approach—and the one I use for new product development—is the process I learned at Arthur D. Little (ADL). At ADL we practiced *breakthrough product development and creation,* which, simply explained, is the introduction of a new product or product feature only when it provides demonstrable value-add to the customer in the form of faster, better and cheaper service, manifesting itself in meaningful amounts of new revenue. Following this formula, a company does NOT develop or introduce marginal products or features and expect new revenue generation. Such marginal new products and features can be used to update existing products and ensure that they remain competitive, but they will not produce new revenue. And new profitable revenue that generates cash and profits is the goal of the turnaround. New products can make huge contributions to revenue generation, assuming the new product development process is operating properly. The formula I use to determine if a product development program is working is that every dollar of capital invested should have a payback in less than three years.

A second way to generate these new products and new revenue is through the search for small tuck-under acquisitions with products that can be tucked under and sold through the TUC's sales infrastructure with no real integration effort. This is an effective and easy-to-implement approach to expanding the product offering and revenue base of the TUC. Of course, the critical issue is to acquire the tuck-under acquisition on a performance or earn-out basis so that the cost of acquisition does not raise the risk profile of the turnaround. This is a good illustration of why it is so important to quickly generate new cash from operations to make it possible to build or acquire new products.

In my opinion, the successful introduction of new products into the sales process and revenue contribution stream is proof-positive the turnaround is succeeding. It not only means new revenues and cash are being generated, but it also demonstrates that an organization is starting to function on an entrepreneurial basis again and is on the offense in the battle for survival.

Phase Four: Optimize!

Figure 9

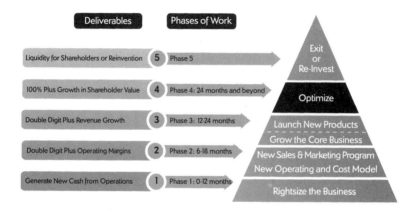

Timeline: Optimization usually begins at the end of the turnaround process and runs through the Exit Phase.

The goal of optimization is to bring all of the key metrics in the business model to their highest possible level of performance. In the service companies that I have turned around, the critical metrics that I focus on to measure optimization and peak performance are as follows:

- Are sales growing at a steady double-digit rate quarter-over-quarter and year-over-year? It's a key, tangible indicator of a successful turnaround if each quarter is ending on a high note, with no borrowing from the next quarter's revenue budget.

- Has EBITDA crossed over the 20 percent of revenue threshold on a quarterly and annual basis? *If a turnaround cannot drive profits to 20 percent, the turnaround has not been successful. This is the key indicator of success.*

- Has the TUC's long-term debt been paid off or substantially reduced as a result of the cash being generated from operations? *Deleveraging the company is another critical indicator of success in a turnaround.*

- Is the company generating at least one major stream of new revenue from a breakthrough product launch each year?

- Are the company's Customer Satisfaction Scores steadily over 95 percent each quarter?

- Is the management team stable and in control of the business and making annual bonuses?

- Are the public or private shareholders happy with the appreciation in their stock, and have they developed new respect for and trust in management?

If the answers to these questions are all "yes," the TUC has been turned and is in optimization mode. This also means that the TUC is ready to enter the final phase of the turnaround and explore an exit, which I will discuss in the next chapter.

An Optimized Management Team

One issue that deserves some special attention in this Optimization Phase is the management team. I enter each TUC with the intention of preserving the management team. I have found that even the best managers can be affected by the poisonous atmosphere in a TUC. So, when I enter the TUC with my turnaround model, turnaround plan and experience, I can breathe new life into what may be considered a bad management team. I have found that strong leadership by an experienced operating CEO—combined with a workable business model, disciplined turnaround philosophy and custom-tailored plan—boosts the effectiveness and overall performance levels of most management teams.

So, for the two years of the turnaround process, *I work to optimize the overall performance of the management team, rather than replacing it at the outset and further disrupting the TUC.* Early on in the process, I can have as many as a dozen direct reports, as I take a personal interest in tutoring and guiding executive managers. I also work an ungodly number of hours and believe in seven-day work weeks at the outset of the turnaround. This establishes a high level of commitment for my team and ensures that those executives who want to improve themselves and are willing to make the sacrifices with me can raise their game and resurrect their careers under my guidance.

New profitable revenue that generates cash and profits is the goal of the turnaround.

I can breathe new life into what may be considered a bad management team.

Unfortunately, not all of the dozen or so executives who report to me at the outset make it. Many just can't keep up with the breakneck pace of the turnaround and/or they don't want to make the commitment required to reverse their own personal fortunes or those of the company. These people usually sort themselves out of the company, and by the end of Phase Three, I generally have six direct reports or executives who have survived the rigorous process.

The surviving management team is very important because it represents the bridge from past poor performance to the better performance the company is currently exhibiting and the promise of optimized future performance. As we enter the Exit Phase and eventual departure of the turnaround executive, this is the leadership upon which new investors or buyers will be counting to drive financial results. They are relying on this team to support investments they have made based on a significantly higher valuation for the TUC than two years earlier when the turnaround process started.

The optimized company performance and the surviving management team are the legacies of the turnaround, which is monetized in Phase Five to create new shareholder wealth. It's crucial to successful monetization that these hearty survivors understand the importance of their role and that they have a stake in the future success of the company. That usually means ensuring leaders have meaningful equity in the form of stock-based compensation in the company, which makes them true investment partners of the shareholders. There's no substitute for this kind of tangible investment in the company's future.

I can't emphasize enough how important it is to make the right decision about the future leadership of the company.

I can't emphasize enough how important it is to make the right decision about the future leadership of the company after I begin to phase out with the shareholders in Phase Five. The wrong decision on the new CEO and the surviving management team can cause the turned-around TUC to lose its momentum and develop performance problems anew.

Here is a checklist of requirements I ask the Board to consider when finding my replacement. (I will—under NO circumstances—participate in the decision on who replaces me. It would give the Board an excuse to avoid doing a thorough search.)

The post-turnaround CEO should:
- Be a hands-on operator of companies, with some financial background
- Have a strong track record for profitably growing businesses
- Be willing to live near and work from the home office (no telecommuters please)
- Be a respected leader of management teams and have a strong work ethic

- Be willing to accept the bulk of compensation on sale of stock at the end of his contract
- Have had at least one major career failure. If the executive hasn't had at least one career failure—something that was of his own making, that kept him awake with cold sweats—he can't really appreciate the responsibility he's taking on in a turnaround. If that's the case, you probably should not hire him.

If these requirements are met, the post-turnaround CEO has a better-than-average chance to continue the momentum and positive performance of the company.

With the management team in place and the new CEO in the wings, we can begin to think about exiting the turnaround process through a sale or merger and guiding the company to the next phase of its life cycle.

8 | Exit and Maximize Shareholder Wealth

Donald Trump, in his book *Think Big and Kick Ass,* expresses the attitude and winning spirit required to do a successful turnaround when he says, "Never do anything for money. Do it for love. To be super-successful you have to love what you are doing. Find a challenge you are passionate about. You will need passion to overcome obstacles, recover from setbacks and make it through tough times. … To be a winner in life find a passion, get out of your comfort zone, be a doer and never give up!"

I carry this attitude with me into every turnaround, along with a commitment to work longer hours, harder and smarter than everyone in the company. *From the minute I walk in the door, failure is not an option, and I will pay almost any price not to fail. However, my golden rule and defining principle is to never fall in love with the company I am turning around because, in the final analysis, getting shareholders paid is the end game.*

From the beginning, I develop a tremendous sense of responsibility and affinity for thousands of shareholders that I have never met; like them, I have a personal stake in making the turnaround work. I think this highly developed sense of accountability goes back to my early childhood and my family's humble beginnings, where every dollar really counted and made a difference in all of our lives. We just could not afford to waste or lose a dollar, and I extend this passion to those shareholders who will lose a great deal of money if I fail. I worry that if I fail, families' pension funds or college tuitions will be lost forever.

(What a sense of fear, accountability, responsibility and—to some degree—anger at the stupidity of the previous stewards of the company rushes through my brain and nervous system!)

Phase Five: Exit

Figure 10

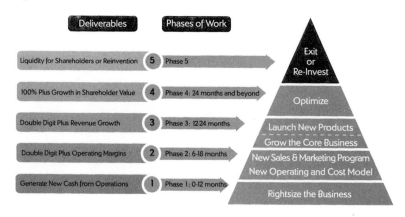

Timeline: Any time after Phase Three is completed and Phase Four optimization has begun.

As a final step, after I have finished the turnaround and restored the lost value to these shareholders, I quickly give shareholders an opportunity to take their money off the table and monetize it through an exit strategy. An exit strategy is usually the sale of the company and a re-capitalization through the new purchaser. To achieve this desired result, the CEO and Board must be able to recognize when shareholder value has reached its peak, exiting current shareholders at that point. Just as importantly, termination forces the Board and shareholders in the acquiring entity to re-capitalize the TUC for future growth—an extremely important concept.

If the reader takes nothing else away from the book, I want the following statement to be tattooed on his brain: *A TUC needs more than a turnaround to survive long term—even one that's been perfectly executed. The TUC must be strengthened across all of its core competencies—and on its balance sheet—by a respectable amount of new capital at some point during the turnaround, or after the turnaround is complete, to successfully make the transition to the next stage of growth.*

Here's why:

During the TUC's decline and two-year turnaround process—while the company was focused on its struggle to survive—markets, technology, competition and a variety of other factors have undoubtedly changed dramatically. Even with improved operations,

I develop a tremendous sense of responsibility and affinity for thousands of shareholders that I have never met.

An equal and opposite force must be applied to stop the decline and reverse the negative momentum.

sales, products and finances, the TUC will have fallen behind the cutting edge of industry and marketplace trends. This is not always apparent to those buried in the details because they are too close and emotionally invested in the turnaround.

The only way for the TUC to return to the cutting edge is through upfront investment of risk capital. Making a bet with its own cash could drastically weaken the company. Therefore, the company must attain new risk capital and resources either through a large, dilutive equity reinvestment from outside shareholders, or by finding a buyer who can make new and better use of updated operations, sales, product and financial resources created in the turnaround.

This is a good place to make an important observation about the human toll of turnarounds: When I enter the company, all the momentum is negative. Management is demoralized; sales and profits are declining; quality is terrible; customers are angry and leaving ... you name it and it is going wrong! To reverse this negative momentum, basic physics comes into play. ***An equal and opposite force must be applied to stop the decline and reverse the negative momentum.*** This force is the mental and physical energy of the new turnaround CEO, newly constituted management team, employees, Board and loyal investors. No matter how smart you are, the physical, mental and emotional effort must be applied by all of the stakeholders and with a force equal to the momentum of the decline, to get the company moving in the right direction again.

Clearly, this intense process is exhausting for investors, Board members and managers who have shouldered the emotional stress of potential failure and financial loss, not to mention shareholder litigation that usually accompanies this corporate crisis. So, when a buyer shows up with fresh capital, ideas and energy, it is usually the right time for the old guard to give way to the new guard.

A couple of final notes on making an exit.

If you haven't considered that litigation could bite you in the b--- just as you think you're making a perfect exit, you deserve to be bitten by the beast. In today's litigation-loony world, there's a good chance something from the TUC's past will surface to create major legal liability for the company—just when you think you've tied up all the loose ends. Thanks to unintended consequences of Sarbanes-Oxley, the problem has significantly intensified in recent years. So every company, and especially public companies, must operate under the specter of a lawsuit causing millions of dollars of legal liability, even if the legal action has no merit.

Considering all of these factors, a major responsibility of the turnaround CEO and the Board is to recognize these issues and—from the early stages of the turnaround—have an exit plan in mind that is designed to maximize and monetize shareholder value.

Maximizing Shareholder Value

The ultimate goal of the turnaround, maximizing shareholder value, has three distinct actions that must accompany a successful operating and financial turnaround.

Investors should target a
100 percent return
on their investment in
two years.

- Investing early to leverage improved financial performance
- Planning a clean exit early to ensure a certain outcome to the turnaround
- Planning for continuity of management and financial performance after the exit

Let's take a deeper look into what these three actions entail.

Investing Early

It's key to the success of the turnaround that investors demonstrate their faith in the turnaround executive and his process by joining him in investing early.

The turnaround CEO invests early by virtue of a compensation package heavily weighted toward payment through the sale of equity at the end of the turnaround process; knowledgeable investors who know the industry know the turnaround CEO and place their bets along with him. These investors recognize the tremendous leverage for returns that exists in TUCs, and the fact that risk can be managed by having a proven turnaround CEO with a proven model. The rule of thumb I use is that investors should target a 100 percent return on their investment in two years.. Under the best conditions, when everything goes right, they can plan on a 200-plus percent return. This has been the case in my last three turnarounds, as shown in the following chart:

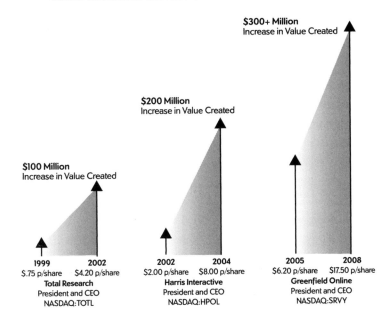

Recent Transactions and Results — Shareholder Value Created

$300+ Million
Increase in Value Created

$200 Million
Increase in Value Created

$100 Million
Increase in Value Created

1999	2002	2002	2004	2005	2008
$.75 p/share	$4.20 p/share	$2.00 p/share	$8.00 p/share	$6.20 p/share	$17.50 p/share
Total Research		**Harris Interactive**		**Greenfield Online**	
President and CEO		President and CEO		President and CEO	
NASDAQ:TOTL		NASDAQ:HPOL		NASDAQ:SRVY	

The reason that such incredible leverage exists is not because of the usual presence of debt. Instead, it is because of the *hidden assets* and the proven turnaround model.

Planning a Clean Exit

We have discussed why an exit strategy is important. However, the turnaround executive must also plan well in advance for a clean exit in order to maximize shareholder value.

An investor can't experience maximization of shareholder value without another investor being willing to buy his stock at the end of the turnaround. Anyone who thinks this event happens naturally does not know the business world or runs his life on luck. The good turnaround CEO is preparing, from day one, a suitable list of strategic and financial buyers who would be willing to pay 200 to 300 percent more for the

TUC than it is worth at day one of the turnaround—recognizing all the hidden value in the company.

It's important to keep a line of communication with these targets always open during the turnaround; you never know when one of these contacts will have a plan that could include acquiring the TUC. And, if a buyer does not show up on its own, I work with an investment bank to initiate—before the Optimization Phase—a competition for the revitalized TUC.

One way or another, a clean exit at the end of the turnaround requires thoughtful planning at the beginning of the turnaround.

Separating the Wheat from the Chaff

(Information taken from article in November 29, 2008, edition of Turnaround Management Association magazine.)

One company that has specialized in separating the wheat from the chaff—zeroing in on TUCs with hidden assets that make them good turnaround candidates—is Sun Capital Partners. One of the investment leaders in the turnaround industry, Sun has invested in and managed more than two hundred companies, in a wide range of industries, since its inception in 1995.

Sun Principal Jason Leach made a key point about investing in turnarounds. "The key to generating substantial IRRs in a turnaround environment is to acquire companies that present opportunities to create enterprise value through operational improvements and expansion in EBITDA. This is more difficult than it sounds. There is a fine line between a turnaround and a liquidation."

The following case studies are perfect approaches to maximizing shareholder wealth.

In May 2003, Owens Corning, a company noted for insulation and other building products, was operating under Chapter 11 protection due to asbestos liability claims. Owens Corning saw a sale of ALSCO Metals Corporation, a wholly owned subsidiary, as an opportunity to exit a non-core metals market. The investment professionals at Sun saw great potential for ALSCO and its 24 percent market share, acquiring ALSCO's assets through a Section 363 bankruptcy sale.

Then Sun set about doing the hard work of a turnaround—cutting costs and reducing working capital investment. It also completed four Six Sigma projects aimed at improving efficiency of coating operations, producing savings of more than $4.3 million.

The numbers really tell the story of the successful turnaround. EBITDA increased from $8 million for the pre-acquisition twelve-month period ending May 2003 to $24.4 million for the twelve months ending September 30, 2005. Then, in October of that year, ALSCO was sold to a publicly traded strategic buyer for a return of more than twenty-one times the original purchase price, with an IRR of about 580 percent.

This is the perfect example of truly maximizing return for shareholders.

The "Blue-light Special" of Clean Exits

The best example I have seen of a well-planned clean exit is the one
Edward S. Lampert executed during the turnaround of Kmart. Lampert
got control of the $23 billion retail chain for less than $1 billion in
bankruptcy court in late 2002. He and his hedge fund ESL became the
largest shareholder after the reorganization and during an ambitious
turnaround plan that reconceptualized the retailer into both a retail
discounter and real estate holdings investment play.

Before the turnaround, Kmart was the poster child of mismanagement.
It was collapsing under the weight of crushing debt. And its approach to
revenue generation was to push up sales numbers to make Wall Street
happy—no matter how little actual profit was generated.

First, Lampert rightsized the company, sending all those mis-managers
off to the unemployment lines. Then he brought in some retail experts—
including a team from The Gap that knew how to find and sell hip, youthful
clothes at bargain prices, thus giving the store a more up-to-date image.
And he decreed that the chain would focus on profit—not sales figures—
selling less, but making more profit. Finally, he leveraged the company's
greatest asset—its real estate. By selling and leasing some of the chain's
prime real estate, Lampert turned useless ghost stores into real income.

The turnaround was executed flawlessly, and the exit was perfect, as
Lampert merged Kmart into Sears for approximately $100 dollars per
share. Not a bad deal for shareholders who had bought the stock out of
reorganization for pennies on the dollar, trusting Lampert to execute the
turnaround. He gave them a clean exit in less than two years.

Continuity of Good Performance After the Exit

The final necessary piece of advanced planning is ensuring continuity of good performance after the exit.

I am 100 percent against turnaround CEOs thinking they can extend their stay at the company by leading it into the next life cycle.

A turnaround CEO must understand that the job is complete at the end of Phase Five, or the exit. I am 100 percent against turnaround CEOs thinking they can extend their stay at the company by leading it into the next life cycle. The next life cycle after exit usually requires a different skill set than that of a turnaround CEO. Therefore, it is best for the turnaround CEO to align his interests with the shareholders and exit when shareholders can monetize the newly enhanced value of their equity in the company.

After the turnaround is complete, the challenge facing the company is how to double its size and move to what I call the *Next Step Function of Growth*. This is a tricky exercise because the business model has been optimized and the company is usually growing steadily at 10 to 12 percent, with 20 percent operating margins. To double the size of the company over a reasonable period (three additional years), growth rates must be accelerated through both organic and external (acquisitions) growth, and margins need to stay respectable, although they will probably drop from 20 percent in the short term. Investment capital is required in order to double the company's size and bring margins back to 20 percent at the end of the three-year period.

The best person for the job in the next phase is a growth-oriented CEO who can take the optimized company and business model I have built and extend it upward. Think of it as putting a second story on the new house that I have built during the turnaround. The new CEO must be an executive who takes measured steps, not a big risk-taker; he should be someone who knows how to use the current structure to continue to build the business. That usually means that he has a background in sales and marketing, with a good, solid understanding of the industry and the strategy that drives it.

Remember that the new buyer will be paying market price for the turned TUC, which will require additional capital and resources to be successful. Therefore, the new buyer will want a management team and CEO capable of executing at high levels of performance into the future. This means that advanced planning must be made in Phase Three of the turnaround to lock the good managers into contracts that will keep them in their jobs through the sale. These managers will undoubtedly benefit financially from the sale, but their real gains must come as a result of their performance for the new buyers.

If these three principles—Investing Early, Planning a Clean Exit and Continuity of Good Performance After the Exit—are recognized and implemented, shareholders will probably monetize their profits when the turnaround CEO leaves the company. If the investors choose not to monetize their newly created shareholder value from the turnaround and roll their investments into the future, their pact with the turnaround CEO is completed and they are on their own.

Dressed in Success
The Warnaco Group, Inc. is a shining example of a company that managed continuity of performance after a turnaround.

In 2001, the company, previously one of the globe's leading apparel companies, filed for bankruptcy, the inevitable result of a crushing debt load, poor financial oversight and inefficient operational management. Global professional services firm Alvarez & Marsal (A&M) came in to affect a turnaround, filling several key positions, including CEO and CFO. The turnaround was so successful it won A&M the prestigious *Turnaround of the Year Award* for 2003 from the Turnaround Management Association. Here's why:

The turnaround executives created a solid financial structure, new accounting controls, disciplined operations and a highly focused business strategy. Following the turnaround, the company's outstanding debt had been reduced from $2.2 billion to $276 million. Creditors received substantial returns, new common stock began trading, and within just a few months, the company closed a $210 million bond offering.

Post-turnaround, the company brought in Joseph Gromek as CEO and Director. The perfect choice as post-turnaround chief executive, he brought to the table incredible industry experience. He'd served as CEO of Brooks Brothers and held senior management positions with Saks Fifth Avenue, Limited Brands, Inc. and Ann Taylor Stores Corporation. He was the right person to keep the company on track post-turnaround.

The Warnaco Group is doing well today, with annual revenue of approximately $2 billion, up nicely over the last few years, and growing profits that are supporting a per-share stock price in the high twenties, with a healthy PE ratio of 13, in today's horrible stock market. The Board at Warnaco got it just right by bringing Gromek in to grow the company after A&M made the turnaround happen. It was a perfect execution of a successful turnaround strategy.

The American Way

In summary, I am frequently criticized for my strict—almost religious—adherence to the belief that the Board, management team and employees all work for the shareholders and that the shareholders MUST make money on their risk capital before we share in the fruits of our labor or equity appreciation in the company. *After all, the fundamental truth of capitalism is that risk capital must be rewarded, or capitalism will cease to be capitalism because the investor will stop investing.*

As an aside, I think the current corporate climate is a perfect reflection of the statement above. Major parts of corporate America have forgotten that their big salaries, stock options, private planes and so on, all must come after rewarding the shareholders by maximizing value. Instead, these leaders view their compensation packages and huge severance programs as entitlements. (What are the Boards and Compensation Committees of these companies thinking?) The result of the wrong-headed thinking speaks for itself: a battlefield of dead or dying American companies.

I personally refuse to go down that path. In every turnaround I undertake, I offer to work for a salary of $1 per year, and I want as much equity in the company as the Board will give me. I want to continue creating wealth for my family and me by maximizing shareholder value and making money when my shareholders make money. It's the American way!

9 In closing …
Rising Out of the Ashes: A New Company with a New Value System

I have built my successful turnaround model over twenty years of trial and error and numerous turnarounds or turnaround situations. Even today, after a very successful turnaround at online media firm Greenfield Online, where we created more than $300 million of new shareholder wealth, I am improving the model and adding the lessons learned over the last two years.

There is little or no theory in the model, just proven work processes that resolve problems and are integrated into a dynamic working model that I can overlay onto almost any troubled company. It works with any company that wants to keep itself out of severe distress or bankruptcy, and that has the will to change its fortunes. I have tried to keep the reading interesting and not too technical, so the book is rich with examples that I hope the reader can relate to in today's environment of bankrupt and near-bankrupt American companies. To say the least, the subject matter of this book is appropriate for our times.

I have not talked about what I call the *spirit of a turnaround effort* and the intrinsic new value system that evolves within a TUC, as the company becomes successful once again and the people begin to believe in themselves, their colleagues and the business.

The spirit of a turnaround is a beautiful thing to watch evolve. It is like a phoenix rising out of the ashes, lifting the spirit of the company and its employees. It is what gives me my greatest joy when the turnaround is complete and success is at hand. It is also the fuel for the energy that takes over within the company after I provide the initial spark for the turnaround. Developing this new spirit within the management and employee infrastructure is a critical variable of the overall turnaround effort. So I watch closely, and if it does not take hold, I know I am doing something wrong as the CEO of the company and leader of the turnaround effort.

Although the concept of a spirit of a turnaround is definitely intangible and hard to visualize, it is very real. It is real because it exists in two distinct value metrics that surface in each of the five phases of the model (AHVCM). Those two value metrics are:

1. Responsibility and Accountability for one's own actions and how those actions impact the organization
2. Adherence to a new value system within the organization, one built on faith in oneself and those supporting you

Without the emergence of these two new value standards in the turnaround, it's impossible to build a healthy, well-functioning organization. Such an organization can't be created out of the classic civil war between individuals and subgroups within the troubled company. The end result of a business built on this foundation would be temporary improvement in the company's performance from the rightsizing in Phase One, then a collapse of the pyramid as I try to rebuild the infrastructure of the company (sales, operations, technology and so on) into a growing, profitable and sustainable business in Phases Two, Three and Four of the pyramid.

Going a little deeper for the reader, I love to refer managers to the book, *The Road Less Traveled,* by Scott Peck, and to his definition of responsibility. Peck writes:

The spirit of a turnaround is like a phoenix rising out of the ashes.

"We cannot solve life's problems except by solving them. This statement may seem self-evident, yet it is seemingly beyond the comprehension of most of the human race. This is because we must accept RESPONSIBILITY for a problem before we solve it. We cannot solve a problem by saying 'It's not my problem.' We cannot solve a problem by hoping someone else will solve it for us. I can only solve a problem when I say this is my problem and it's up to me to solve it. ... But many, so many, seek to avoid the pain of their problems by saying to themselves, 'This problem was caused by other people and circumstances beyond my control and therefore it is up to other people to solve this problem for me. ...'"

The point is that the new value system emerging from the turnaround should reverse the negative energy within the company. No longer should people try to avoid accountability for problem solving. Instead, there should be the positive energy that comes from individuals embracing responsibility, proactively solving problems and moving the company upward through the pyramid to success.

This embracing of responsibility and problem solving is possible because the once-demoralized employees see that they can solve problems and succeed, even when everyone else thinks they will fail—or wants them to fail. This is a major change in the underlying execution capabilities of the company and it starts with me. In fact, I like to tell people that everything begins with faith. I define faith as ***the substance of things hoped for and the belief in the things not yet seen.*** I tell people that I never take on a turnaround that I do not think will succeed but that I just cannot tell them how exactly it will happen. However, I have faith in myself, my model and them and that is enough to get the job done. When the employees see at the outset the faith I have in myself, my model and them, I've sown the seeds of a *Can Do* mentality.

I like to refer people to this quote by Thomas Watson Jr., one of IBM's great leaders. "The basic spirit, philosophy and energy of an organization have more to do with its success and achievements than do the technological, economic and other material resources at its disposal. ... All of these material resources are transcended by how strongly the people in the organization believe in the company and how faithfully they carry out their roles and responsibilities." This is the spirit on which IBM was built and what made it the success it is today. I help people at TUCs believe that, if it worked at IBM, it will work for our turnaround and in their company.

> The new value system emerging from the turnaround should reverse the negative energy within the company.

So, in the **END**, a turnaround of a TUC can best be summed up as: *the phoenix rising out of the ashes, with a new sense of itself and its basic values of responsibility and faith, supported by a proven turnaround model and led by a leader and management team who will not accept failure as an option.* They will find a way to achieve success for the shareholders, managers and employees of the once-troubled company. This is the goal I strive for in every turnaround.